THE RISE AND FALL OF CIVILIZATION

THE RISE AND FALL OF CIVILIZATION

From Creation through the Flood

DAVID HOCKING

MULTNOMAH

Portland, Oregon 97266

Unless otherwise indicated, all Scripture references are from the Holy Bible, New King James Version, © 1982, 1984 by Thomas Nelson, Inc.

Cover design by Krieg Barrie

THE RISE AND FALL OF CIVILIZATION
© 1989 by Calvary Communications, Inc.
Published by Multnomah Press
Portland, Oregon 97266

Multnomah Press is a ministry of Multnomah School of the Bible, 8435 Northeast Glisan Street, Portland, Oregon 97220.

Printed in the United States of America

Library of Congress Cataloging-in-Publication Data

Hocking, David L.
    The rise and fall of civilization: from creation through the flood/David Hocking.
        p. cm.
    Bibliography: p.
    ISBN 0-88070-308-3
    1. Bible. O.T. Genesis I, 1-IX, 19—Commentaries. I. Title.
BS1235.3.H63   1989
222'.1107—dc19   89-31381
                                                  C I P

89 90 91 92 93 94 95 96 - 10 9 8 7 6 5 4 3 2 1

Contents

Introduction

Watching my wife give birth to our first child started me to think. A trip to the Griffith Park Observatory in Los Angeles kept the quest alive. When and where did life begin? What caused the galaxies, our own solar system? The questions are many; the answers more complex and disturbing.

Maybe a friend was right when he said to me, "Who cares? I have to go to work in the morning!" Many of us do not want to face the ultimate issues of life, death, and eternity. They require diligent study and intellectual honesty that seem so rare in a narcissistic culture pursuing questions of self-worth and personal happiness.

Down deep in the isolation of my own thoughts has been a growing awareness that the matter of origins is vitally related to one's sense of purpose, worth, and meaning in life. Finding out the roots of the Hocking name (a pursuit for which I paid a few shekels!) was interesting, but not completely satisfying. Do we all go back to Adam and Eve, as the Bible indicates? Did life and history begin again after the flood with Noah, his three sons, and their wives? Is Abraham the father of us all? Are these merely religious questions that have no tangible proof within the sciences known to the human race?

Scientists seem sure that our solar system is billions of years old and that dinosaurs disappeared some sixty-three million years ago. Their explanations of the origin of all things have been far from conclusive. Proof is lacking but theories abound. Did everything that we know today come from a "big bang," a chemical reaction that caused our world to come into existence? Are we really related to apes?

Introduction

These questions and many like them have inspired me to research and reflect deeply upon the biblical record of origins. That record stands in stunning simplicity when compared to human attempts to explain the origin of all things. The first book of the Bible is called "Genesis," a Greek word for "beginning." Its opening words are "In the beginning." What a good place to start!

If you enjoy the challenge of viewpoints about origins, the biblical account will give you much food for thought. Here's hoping you will find it stimulating and provocative, as well as rewarding.

Who Wrote the Book of Genesis?

My Bible says that Genesis is the "first book of Moses," although that is an editorial remark not found in the actual text of the first five books. Apparently Moses wrote five books, not counting the last few verses of Deuteronomy which record his death. His friend Joshua no doubt penned those words (cf. Deuteronomy 34:5-12 and Joshua 1:1-5).

Some scholars claim that Moses could not have written the first five books of the Bible. They argue that he served as a collector of oral traditions and mythological writings of various ancient cultures that often speak about the origin of life and history. They suppose that there were several sources from which he compiled these books.

In contrast to these opinions, the New Testament claims that Jesus Christ believed Moses to be the author of statements found in Genesis as well as in the rest of the Old Testament law (Matthew 8:4; 19:7-8; Mark 1:44; 7:10; Luke 24:27, 44; John 5:45-47).

Although there is a great deal of disagreement about the date of Moses (between the fifteenth and thirteenth century B.C.), there is no reason to question his authorship of the first five books of the Bible (the Pentateuch) or the law (or Torah, the title Jewish people prefer). My studies have convinced me that Moses lived in the fifteenth century B.C. and the exodus from Egypt took place around 1446 B.C.

In spite of the great knowledge and ability of Moses (see Acts 7:22), the only way he could write about the origins of life and history was if God gave him this information directly. The Bible says that God spoke "in time past to the fathers by the prophets"

(Hebrews 1:1). Second Peter 1:20-21 reveals how the human writers were able to write the Bible: "knowing this first, that no prophecy of Scripture is of any private interpretation, for prophecy never came by the will of man, but holy men of God spoke as they were moved by the Holy Spirit."

Whether you believe this is how it happened or not, it is important to recognize the direct intervention of God Himself according to the Bible. God spoke and directly communicated to certain "prophets" what He wanted the human race to hear and know. They were simply mouthpieces to tell the people exactly what God said. No free translations were allowed!

Does this mean that God speaks to us today by the same method, through chosen prophets? While some religious groups argue that possibility, the Bible teaches the opposite. The biblical record is a sufficient statement from God. He has told us all that He wants us to know and, in turn, holds us accountable for it. Hebrews 1:1-2 is clear:

> God, who at various times and in different ways
> spoke in time past to the fathers by the prophets, has
> in these last days spoken to us by His Son, whom He
> has appointed heir of all things, through whom also
> He made the worlds.

God spoke through these prophets "in time past," suggesting that this method is no longer used. The phrase "in these last days" can be translated "in the last of these days," that is, the days in which the prophets communicated the words of God verbally to the people. The "last" of such prophetic utterances was to occur at the time of Jesus Christ, God's final revelation to humanity, whose life, teachings, miracles, death, resurrection, and predictions are found within the pages of the New Testament.

The final book of the New Testament claims to be the final word about Jesus Christ. Revelation 22:18-19 warns that no one is to add to these words or take away from them. To do otherwise is to face eternal consequences.

Do Genesis and Science Agree?

This is a tough question. Science observes facts and is not designed to interpret the facts, although many scientists find themselves doing just that. Science has many presuppositions that force us into a difficult spot when we come to the Bible. Likewise, it is difficult for science to tackle the religious issues involved with the study of origins which the Bible presents. Are the two compatible? Yes and no.

Yes, if you mean are the facts of the Bible scientifically possible, and yes, if you mean are the observable facts of the universe pointing to a Creator or a Designer. But the answer is no if you mean that the interpretations of science (such as evolution) are compatible with the record of Genesis. The plain truth from a simple reading of the Genesis account is that the Bible is in direct conflict with the hypotheses of evolutionary thought.

So where does that lead us? I hope it will lead us into more careful study of the facts, both within the physical and material universe and within the Bible itself. Whatever the real facts are about the universe, there are many of us who believe that it is impossible for them to conflict with biblical teaching. To some observers, such loyalty to the biblical record leads to a closed mind. Such need not be the case. The problem is this: The God Who claims ownership of the Bible is the same God (according to the Bible) Who created the heavens and the earth. His revelation in the universe cannot contradict His revelation in the written record of the Bible. To believe otherwise is to present yourself with an unsolvable mystery and an intellectual contradiction that would leave the best of us in utter despair and frustration. God, because of Who He is, obviously cannot contradict Himself in anything that He has said or done.

One possible way out of this problem is to deny the existence of God and the reliability of the Genesis account. Many have chosen this route, but it leaves us with tremendous questions and impossibilities. Those who hold this position do not seem concerned since, in their view, it is only a question of time until we figure out the ultimate origin of all things. They prefer to wait. This viewpoint also relieves them of any responsibility or accountability to God since they do not believe He exists.

Another possible viewpoint is that the human authors of the Bible are mistaken about origins. This view argues that God should not be blamed for what the human authors understood or communicated. The problem with this view is that it removes God's protection and ability to guarantee the accuracy of the written record, which claims that God has inspired it and directly revealed it.

So our problem is this: Do we argue for a cosmology that leaves God out? Do we try to resolve this dilemma by speaking of the accurate revelation of God in the physical and material universe, and the fallible information of the Bible due to the inadequacies of human authorship? Or, do we accept the biblical record as totally accurate and reliable and trust that the scientific evidence produced by the study of the physical and material universe will one day confirm what the Bible has said about origins? Hasn't science been wrong about the physical evidence before? Did we not once argue that the world was flat instead of round, that our solar system was geocentric instead of heliocentric?

At this point, we need to be up-front about the viewpoint of this study. In approaching the study of origins in the book of Genesis, we will begin with the following assumptions (taking for granted that you may not agree!):

1. The Bible is the inerrant Word of God (there are no mistakes).

2. The Bible gives correct information about the origin of all things.

3. The Bible, though scientifically accurate in its statements, is not a textbook on science. It is written from the viewpoint of common people, living on planet earth.

4. God created the heavens and the earth and everything that lives.

5. The purpose of God's creation is to reveal the character and power of God Himself and to motivate all of His creation to worship Him.

With these assumptions in view, let's take a closer look at what happened "in the beginning."

Chapter 1
In the Beginning
(1:1-2)

Trying to understand a time when there was nothing is a seemingly impossible task for a finite mind. The Bible begins with the phrase "In the beginning," and expects us to accept that sublime, simple thought about the origin of everything.

From a rational point of view, the sequence of events reminds us that somewhere, at sometime, all things had a beginning. Conceiving of that moment is our problem.

It is of some interest that the Bible does not begin with arguments about the existence of God. It assumes that fact and quickly moves to what God has done.

The word *genesis* is the Greek word for "beginning," although this first book of the Bible was originally written in Hebrew. It is the title found in the Septuagint, the Greek translation of the Hebrew Scriptures, completed by seventy Jewish scholars over a hundred years before the time of Jesus Christ. The whole book is about the beginnings of the universe, time, human life, history, nations, families. It tells us where we have come from and why we are here.

The Origin of All Things
(1:1-2)

The opening words of the first two verses of Genesis contain a simple, but comprehensive statement on the origin of all things:

¹In the beginning God created the heavens and the earth. ²The earth was without form, and void; and

> **darkness was on the face of the deep. And the Spirit
> of God was hovering over the face of the waters.**

Creation Is a Revelation of the Glory of God

The words "God created the heavens and the earth" reveal much about the nature and attributes of God. The very name *God* appears thirty-two times in the first chapter of Genesis alone! This is the story of what God did.

Psalm 19:1-4 expresses the fact that creation reveals God's glory (cf. Psalm 97:6):

> The heavens declare the glory of God;
> And the firmament shows His handiwork.
> Day unto day utters speech,
> And night unto night reveals knowledge.
> There is no speech nor language
> Where their voice is not heard.
> Their line has gone out through all the earth,
> And their words to the end of the world.

The word *God* is a plural form in Hebrew (*'ĕlōhîm*), but the word *created* is a singular form. Some speak of God's name in the plural as a way to emphasize His greatness. It is sometimes called a "majestic plural." Others believe that the plural form suggests that God consists of more than one person. Christians speak of the "tri-unity" of God, meaning that there is One God made up of three distinct persons: Father, Son, and Holy Spirit.

Several things are revealed about God's glory in these opening words of Genesis.

His obvious preexistence is revealed ("in the beginning"). God was there before anything material existed. All that God did in creating, He accomplished out of nothing. The Hebrew word for *created* (*bārā'*) refers to the incomparable creative activity of God and lends itself well to the concept of creating something out of nothing. No previously existing materials were used. Psalm 90:1-2 says of God:

> LORD, You have been our dwelling place in all
>   generations.
> Before the mountains were brought forth,
> Or ever You had formed the earth and the world,
> Even from everlasting to everlasting, You are God.

The viewpoint of the Bible is that before anything existed, there was God and God alone!

His future purpose is revealed ("the earth was without form and void"). The earth is mentioned as a creation of God along with the heavens. No other planets receive such attention. The earth is the unique dwelling place that God designed for the creature He would make out of the dust of the ground. However, immediately after the moment of bringing the heavens and the earth into existence, the Genesis record tells us that the condition of the earth was "without form and void." These Hebrew words (*tōhû* and *bōhû*) can also be found in Jeremiah 4:23-26:

> I beheld the earth, and indeed it was without form,
>   and void;
> And the heavens, they had no light,
> I beheld the mountains, and indeed they trembled,
> And all the hills moved back and forth.
> I beheld, and indeed there was no man,
> And all the birds of the heavens had fled.
> I beheld, and indeed the fruitful land was a
>   wilderness,
> And all its cities were broken down
> At the presence of the LORD,
> By His fierce anger.

Though speaking in the context of the judgment of the Lord, we get an idea of the meaning of the words "without form and void." It refers to that which is empty, no inhabitants and no sign of life, vegetation, or beautiful surroundings.

The words imply that more is to come and suggest the future purpose of God. It reminds us that earth is the unique place of God's creation with man as the center of it all. God's purpose does not center in a material universe alone, but uniquely in the human race, for which earth was designed.

Did Something Terrible Happen to Planet Earth?

Many theologians and scientists see a catastrophe in the words "without form and void." To them these words indicate a chaotic condition, possibly a world filled with mutation and ugliness, perhaps the period of the dinosaurs. Their viewpoint centers on two biblical passages that speak about the fall of Lucifer (Isaiah 14:12-15), a name given to the king of Babylon, whose ultimate destruction is being prophesied, and the fall of an anointed cherub (Ezekiel 28:12-19), a title given to the king of Tyre.

According to this theory (called "the gap theory" since it argues that a gap exists between Genesis 1:1 and 1:2), the real personage behind the kings of Babylon and Tyre is Satan himself. This theory holds that the fall of Satan (referred to in Revelation 12:7-12) from a position of glory in God's heaven occurs between Genesis 1:1 and 1:2 and results in a chaotic world, brought about by the devil's influence.

One motivating factor behind this theory is an attempt to explain the arguments of evolution within the context of the Genesis account. This chaotic world could have been the domain of the dinosaurs and perhaps a pre-Adamic race of people with apelike characteristics, such as those which evolutionary paleontologists continue to discover and proclaim to be millions of years old.

Most adherents of the gap theory argue for the validity of their theory based on the following four points:

1. The word *was* at the beginning of Genesis 1:2 could be translated "became," thus indicating a change in condition;

2. The words "without form and void" refer to judgment in Jeremiah 4:23-26, and should be treated the same in Genesis 1:2;

3. The word *darkness* in Genesis 1:2 is a frequent symbol of evil in the Bible and should be regarded as such in this passage;

4. The word *fill* in Genesis 1:28 could be translated "refill" or "replenish," thus indicating that there was a population previous to Adam and Eve.

Are these arguments valid? Although interesting, it would seem to the average reader of the Genesis account that there should be more in the text if, in fact, such a catastrophe really occurred.

The first argument concerning the word *was* being translated as *became* requires that the Hebrew lettering called a "*waw*" be a "*waw* consecutive," indicating a subsequent event. However, it appears that it is not a "*waw* consecutive," but rather a "*waw* disjunctive," which means that the phrase "without form and void" describes the preceding clause, not that which happens subsequently to the statement of Genesis 1:1.

The second argument is possible, but it is also quite probable that the point of the words is to emphasize the result of the judgment not simply the fact of judgment. Thus, the argument is lost.

The third argument about "darkness" is interesting, but not conclusive. Job 38:19-21 speaks of it in a positive light, the result of the creative work of God. When God created the heavens and the earth, there was no evil present. The word *darkness* is simply the opposite of light. While it is true that the Bible uses the word as a metaphor for evil or sin, it does not always do so. To see darkness in Genesis 1:2 as a reference to evil is a case of eisegesis (reading into the text), not exegesis (letting the text speak for itself). Genesis 1:5 says that God called the darkness "night." That's the point, nothing more.

The fourth argument is not valid. The word *fill* is translated correctly and simply urges Adam and Eve to propagate the race and to fill the planet with people.

The conclusion? There is no gap between Genesis 1:1 and 1:2. The words "without form and void" speak of the earth as a sphere without shape or design—it is empty and uninhabited, awaiting the days of creation to fill it with beauty and life.

The opening words of Genesis speak of a future purpose of God that centers in the creation of man. The planet was designed to be his dwelling place, and the heavens a reminder of the God Who placed man on the earth. Psalm 8:3-4 states:

> When I consider Your heavens, the work of Your
>   fingers,
> The moon and the stars, which You have ordained,
> What is man that You are mindful of him,
> And the son of man that You visit him?

His active presence is revealed ("and the Spirit of God was hovering over the face of the waters"). Deuteronomy 32:11-12 likens the Lord's care of His people to that of an eagle which "hovers over" its young ones. The active presence of the Spirit of God in creation is clearly evident in these opening words of Genesis. Job 26:13 adds, "By His Spirit He adorned the heavens."

All three persons of the Godhead (Father, Son, and Holy Spirit) were active in the creation of all things. John 1:3 makes this remarkable statement about Jesus Christ: "All things were made through Him, and without Him nothing was made that was made."

Creation Is a Result of the Greatness of God

I never cease to be amazed at the stellar heavens. Millions of stars filling the galaxies, including our own. The nearest star some four light years away (light traveling at a speed of 186,000 miles a second), and Psalm 147:4 says that God "counts the number of the stars; He calls them all by name." Incredible! Whoever created outer space with all of its solar systems has to be a force of incredible power.

God's greatness is incomprehensible to us. Apparently there are no limitations upon His power and resources (Psalm 147:5). The psalmist frequently urges us to praise the greatness of our God (Psalm 48:1), especially as we view His work of creation.

Creation demonstrates the power of His Word. Ten times in the creation story we read "And God said." Psalm 33 makes it abundantly clear:

> By the word of the LORD the heavens were made,
> And all the host of them by the breath of His mouth.
> . . . .
> For He spoke, and it was done;
> He commanded, and it stood fast.
>
> (vv. 6, 9)

His words sustain the stellar heavens as well as bring them all into existence (Isaiah 40:26). What incredible power behind the simple word of God (Psalm 148:1-6)! God said it, and it happened.

The very Word of God that brought the galaxies and our planet into reality and physical form is the same Word that can change human hearts and bring new life from God:

> Having been born again, not of corruptible seed but incorruptible, through the word of God which lives and abides forever, because
> "All flesh is as grass,
> And all the glory of man as the flower of the grass.
> The grass withers,
> And its flower falls away;
> But the word of the LORD endures forever."
>
> (1 Peter 1:23-25)

God's Word is the powerful "incorruptible seed" which lasts forever. Being "born again" or becoming "new creatures in Christ" (2 Corinthians 5:17) occurs because of the power of God's Word. Romans 10:17 states, "So then faith comes by hearing, and hearing by the word of God."

Creation discloses the extent of His power. The size of the universe, its multiple galaxies, tells us much about the extent of the power of God. It appears to be limitless. No wonder the Lord said to Abraham about the ability of his aged and barren wife, Sarah, to have a child, "Is anything too hard for the LORD?" (Genesis 18:14).

The extent of God's power causes all of us to stop and think when we confront passages in the Bible like Ephesians 3:20-21:

> Now to Him who is able to do exceedingly abundantly above all that we ask or think, according to the power that works in us, to Him be glory in the church by Christ Jesus throughout all ages, world without end. Amen.

Astronomers can calculate the size of the universe. Just using the velocity of light, the size of the present known universe requires that it be at least twenty billion years old! Of course, that does not mean it is that old, for God could have created the universe with the appearance of age and could have sent its light in all directions at once and filled it immediately with light. But the size of the universe still requires billions of years for us to observe it. What an amazing fact about the power of God. Job 11:7-9 says:

> Can you search out the deep things of God?
> Can you find out the limits of the Almighty?
> They are higher than heaven—what can you do?
> Deeper than Sheol—what can you know?
> Their measure is longer than the earth
> And broader than the sea.

This passage in the book of Job contrasts the finite ability of man with the infinite power of God. Creation emphasizes the extent of God's power and should motivate us all to acknowledge that God is able to do great and mighty things and that our need is to trust and depend upon Him.

Creation demands faith on our part. Listening to scholars in various fields of science discuss the origin of our solar system and the galaxies of outer space is indeed a stimulating experience. Yet it can also be quite frustrating, for science is incapable of answering with certainty questions about the original cause of the universe. From a rational point of view, the existence of creation demands something more than reason and intellectual skills from the best of us. Creation stands as a constant reminder to all of us that faith is required, a commodity greatly lacking in the majority of us who live in a world of things that we can see, handle, or design.

The Bible assumes man's inability to understand the creation and to fathom its beginnings. Notice God's pointed words in His confrontation with Job (38:4-7):

> Where were you when I laid the foundations of the
>   earth?
> Tell Me, if you have understanding.
> Who determined its measurements?
> Surely you know!
> Or who stretched the line upon it?
> To what were its foundations fastened?
> Or who laid its cornerstone,
> When the morning stars sang together,
> And all the sons of God shouted for joy?

The writer of Hebrews declares clearly that belief in the biblical account of creation demands simple faith on our part (Hebrews 11:1-3, italics mine):

> Now faith is the substance of things hoped for, the evidence of things not seen. For by it the elders obtained a good testimony. *By faith* we understand that the worlds were framed by the word of God, so that the things which are seen were not made of things which are visible.

When the argument is presented that the universe is the product of the spoken word of God, it requires faith. Yet faith needs an object. It is not simply "whistling in the dark," or hoping that something is so when there are no facts available to substantiate what one believes. The object of faith, that which we are to trust, is the "word of God." The Bible itself states quite emphatically that God simply spoke the words and the creation of the universe came into being. We either believe what the

Bible is saying about the origin of all things, or we don't.

Some scholars believe the study of cosmology reveals that there was a Creator. It is helpful to hear such evidence, but the bottom line is that faith is required, no matter what our view of the origin of all things. In some respects, the more simple view is to accept the presence and existence of God as the Beginner of the beginning of all things.

Creation Is a Reflection of the Goodness of God

God's greatness points to His power, whereas His goodness speaks of His plan. Seven times in Genesis 1 we read that what God created was "good." In Genesis 1:31, summarizing all that had taken place, God declared it to be "very good." God's creation was good in two senses. It was good because of what it was intended to do or achieve (its purpose), and it was good because it was intrinsically good, not evil or worthless (its nature).

The God of creation is the God of providence, controlling and sustaining the events of His design for the ultimate good and blessing of the creatures He loves and calls to Himself. Psalm 107:21-22 invites us to be thankful for His providential care:

> Oh, that men would give thanks to the LORD for His
> goodness,
> And for His wonderful works to the children of men!
> Let them sacrifice the sacrifices of thanksgiving,
> And declare His works with rejoicing.

This wonderful refrain in Psalm 107 urges us to give thanks to the Lord for His wonderful works. It appears in verses 8, 15, 21, and 31. What the "wonderful works" of God display is His goodness. The psalmist echoes that thought scores of times by saying "the Lord is good."

God's goodness is reflected in creation in at least two basic ways:

The immutability of His plan. God's creation reveals that He does not change. He is totally reliable like the order of His universe. Even though creation will not endure forever in its present state, God remains the same. He is the unchangeable God (Psalm 102:25-28; James 1:17). What comfort to our hearts to know that our God is totally reliable and unchanging in His essential nature and in the exercise of His attributes and plan!

Psalm 89:33-37 expresses this truth in beautiful and comforting words for the people of Israel:

> Nevertheless My lovingkindness I will not utterly take
>   from him,
> Nor allow My faithfulness to fail.
> My covenant I will not break,
> Nor alter the word that has gone out of My lips.
> Once I have sworn by My holiness;
> I will not lie to David:
> His seed shall endure forever,
> And his throne as the sun before Me;
> It shall be established forever like the moon,
> Even like the faithful witness in the sky.

God's goodness is reflected in the immutability of His promises, reliable like the "faithful witness in the sky," perhaps a reference to the rainbow and God's promise to Noah that He would never again destroy the world with a flood.

The intention behind His plan. God's ultimate purpose in creation is also a reflection of His goodness. He desires us to praise and worship Him, to give Him thanks for all things. A practical example of such goodness and its stated purpose is found in 1 Timothy 4:1, 3-5:

> Now the Spirit expressly says that in latter times some will depart from the faith . . . commanding to abstain from foods which God created to be received with thanksgiving by those who believe and know the truth. For every creature of God is good and nothing is to be refused if it is received with thanksgiving; for it is sanctified by the word of God and prayer.

What God has created is "sanctified [set apart] by the word of God and prayer." It is set apart for its proper use by what the Bible says about it, and by our prayers of thanksgiving to God for the goodness which these "foods" reflect. That is a strong reason for always praying a prayer of thanksgiving at every meal we eat. It recognizes the intention of God's plan in creating all things in the beginning. Creation, including the foods we eat, reflects His goodness and motivates us to give Him thanks.

Creation Is a Reminder of the Grace of God

The glory of God reveals His person; the greatness of God reveals His power; the goodness of God reveals His plan; but the grace of God reveals His purpose.

Grace gives us what we do not deserve nor can achieve on our own. Humanity has no capacity whatsoever to create out of nothing. We design with previously existing materials. God's creation reminds us that He is a God of grace, giving us what we cannot do or achieve on our own.

Creation gives us what belongs to Him to enjoy. It all belongs to God (Psalm 89:11). And yet, these words from Psalm 115:14-16 reveal the grace of God–giving us what already belongs to Him to enjoy:

> May the LORD give you increase more and more,
> You and your children.
> May you be blessed by the LORD,
> Who made heaven and earth.
> The heaven, even the heavens, are the LORD's;
> But the earth He has given to the children of men.

It all belongs to God, but it is given to us to enjoy. These verses pray for the blessing of the God of creation upon His creatures. God gives the earth to us to enjoy—what an incredible reminder of His grace, giving us what we do not deserve nor could ever achieve on our own.

Creation motivates us to worship Him. In Nehemiah 9, the Levites lead the people of Israel in the worship of God because of His creation:

> Blessed be Your glorious name,
> Which is exalted above all blessing and praise!
> You alone are the LORD;
> You have made heaven,
> The heaven of heavens, with all their host,
> The earth and all things on it,
> The seas and all that is in them,
> And You preserve them all.
> The host of heaven worships you.
>
> (vv. 5b-6)

In the Beginning

Does creation remind you of the grace of God and motivate you to worship Him? He gave us what we did not deserve, what we could not achieve, what we could not design by our own skills or ingenuity. God's original purpose in creation is our enjoyment of what He has made and our worship for what He has made.

In the traffic of southern California, my patience often runs thin. Time is so precious and it seems such a waste to spend it on a crowded freeway. While enduring these frequent moments of frustration one morning, I happened to take a long look at the mountains that surround the area's megalopolis. It was one of those rare, clear days, and the sun's rays behind the mountains just seemed to radiate grandeur and beauty—it was a quiet reminder of the creative hand of Almighty God, and it motivated me in the midst of thousands of cars to offer praise and thanksgiving to God for what He has displayed in the world around us.

When was the last time you smelled the flowers, admired the trees, and rejoiced in the realms of outer space with their millions of stars? God's creation tells us much about His glory, power, kindness, and ultimate purposes. Take some time right now to at least think about it. Better yet, put the book down, go outside, take a deep breath, and enjoy what God has made, giving a word of thanks to Him from your heart!

Chapter 2

Creation in Six Days?

(1:1-2:3)

Did God really create everything in six twenty-four-hour days? The Bible's account of the origin of all things is indeed simple. A child can easily read it and understand that God did it. But is it true? How can we reconcile the simple statements of Genesis 1 with the findings of science? Evidence of process requiring millions, perhaps billions, of years causes many to doubt the accuracy and reliability of the biblical account.

The Days of Creation Display the Wonderful Work of God

From Genesis 1:1 to 2:3, the word *God* appears thirty-five times. If we say anything about the creation account in the Bible, we must say that it displays the work of God Himself (Psalm 19:1-4). When we think of creation as the work of God, we conclude two basic things: It was original, and it was complete.

Creation by God was original. The Hebrew word *bārā'* is used thirty-three times in the Bible and appears in the creation account in the following places:

1:1 In the beginning God *created* the heavens and the earth.

1:21 So God *created* great sea creatures and every living thing that moves, with which the waters abounded, according to their kind, and every winged bird according to its kind.

1:27 So God *created* man in His own image; in the image of God He *created* him; male and female He *created* them.

2:3   Then God blessed the seventh day and sanctified it, because in it He rested from all His work which God had *created* and made.

The basic meaning of *bārā'* is "to create," and the word is used only of God's creative work; what He made was indeed original. Hebrews 11:3 tells us: "By faith we understand that the worlds were framed by the word of God, so that the things which are seen were not made of things which are visible. "

The creation account also uses the Hebrew word *`āsâ* ("to do" or "to make") to express what God did during the days of creation. Both *`āsâ* and *bārā'* reinforce our understanding that all the days of creation display the wonderful work of God. His creation was original—no previously existing materials were used.

Creation by God was complete. When God created, nothing was unfinished or needing repair. Much of what I try to make looks like something is missing or that more needs to be done. Not so with God!

Genesis 2:1 contains a simple but powerful statement: "Thus the heavens and the earth, and all the host of them, were finished." To argue otherwise is to deny what the Bible obviously says. Everything was finished within the six days of God's creative work.

The Days of Creation Disagree with Many Conclusions and Arguments of Evolution

It is pointless to avoid the conflict between the arguments of the biblical account of creation and those of the theory of evolution. A simple reading reveals the two are incompatible, though there are scientists and theologians who are working hard on trying to reconcile the two viewpoints.

We should always be open to new discoveries and additional information, refusing to suppress scientific research or academic pursuit. On the other hand, we must also face the facts as we know them. At the present time, the Bible's account of the origin of all things is not compatible with the conclusions of evolution. That fact can be seen in at least three ways.

The origin of all things—a major point of disagreement. Evolution is not on a crusade to prove the existence and power of God. While many scientists and theologians see no problem here and even speak of "theistic evolution," the facts are that the chief proponents of evolutionary thinking in our world do not believe in the existence of a personal God as described in the Bible.

The Bible says "In the beginning God created." Nothing else was involved but God. The Bible describes in marvelous detail the nature, attributes, and works of the God of creation. Evolutionists may talk of an original cause or force which began the processes of evolution that now result in our present universe and all its forms of life; but the personal God of the Bible is not their idea of the original cause or force.

The Bible describes those who deny the existence of God as "wicked" and "foolish" (Psalm 10:4, 14:1). One of the most graphic descriptions of man's wickedness in rejecting God as the Creator is found in Romans 1:18-32. The opening verses of that extended passage reveal the problem:

> For the wrath of God is revealed from heaven against all ungodliness and unrighteousness of men, who suppress the truth in unrighteousness, because what may be known of God is manifest in them, for God has shown it to them. For since the creation of the world His invisible attributes are clearly seen, being understood by the things that are made, even His eternal power and Godhead, so that they are without excuse, because, although they knew God, they did not glorify Him as God, nor were thankful, but became futile in their thoughts, and their foolish hearts were darkened. Professing to be wise, they became fools, and changed the glory of the incorruptible God into an image made like corruptible man—and birds and four-footed beasts and creeping things.

The final verse of Romans 1 (v. 32) reveals that the attitudes and actions of those who "suppress" (v. 18) the knowledge of God in creation deserve the "righteous judgment of God."

The order in which all things came into existence—an apparent part of the disagreement. The word *apparent* is important. Some scientists believe the order of things in the Genesis account can be reconciled with the present knowledge of science and its theories of evolution if the "days" of creation are considered to be long periods of time and not twenty-four-hour days. More about that problem later.

But, can the order of events in the Genesis account of creation be reconciled with the present viewpoints of evolution? John Skinner, principal and professor of Old Testament language and literature at Westminster College in Cambridge, wrote long ago (1910), "The order in which the various living forms are created, the manner in which they are grouped, and their whole development compressed into special periods, are all opposed to geological evidence."

A few of the problems relating to the order of things include:

1. The opening statement about the creation of the heavens and the earth with the making of the sun, moon, and stars on the fourth day.

2. The creation of "light" on the first day with the making of "lights" on the fourth day.

3. The creation of plant life on the third day with the making of the sun on the fourth day. How can plant life survive without the sun?

4. The creation of "trees" on the third day coming before the creation of marine organisms on the fifth day. Evolution teaches the opposite.

5. Plants created as mature, self-producing biological units, containing their own seeds. Impossible for evolution to accept.

6. The creation of the "firmament" called "heaven" on the second day when the opening verse speaks of the "heavens" already in existence and "lights" being placed in the "firmament of the heavens" on the fourth day.

These problems are simply examples of the "apparent" disagreement which science has with the biblical account. Some try to resolve the difficulty by denying the scientific accuracy of the biblical record, believing that it portrays a simple but beautiful presentation of the universe as man understood it over three thousand years ago. With the knowledge available to us today, we have a distinct advantage in evaluating the accuracy of the biblical account.

Many scientists and theologians believe the answer lies in what has been described as "progressive creationism." This view necessitates the days of creation being taken as geological periods, each day representing millions of years.

After reading and examining many of the explanations of both science and religion, and then returning to a simple reading of the Genesis account of creation, I feel compelled to repeat the point we began with: The days of creation disagree with many conclusions and explanations of evolution concerning the origin of all things as well as the order in which the biblical account presents it.

The opportunity for all things to be created within six days—a serious disagreement with evolution. It is over this point that we see the greatest opposition with the viewpoints of modern science. They speak in terms of millions, even billions, of years; the biblical account seems to present a very young earth (thousands of years) if the days are twenty-four-hour periods of time.

Reasons for the Days of Creation Being Geological Ages

The apparent age of the solar system. Astronomy indicates the age of the solar system must involve billions of years. Given the vastness of space, the time required for light to reach us from distant galaxies, even with that light traveling at 186,000 miles a second, would require much more time than thousands of years.

The apparent age of planet earth. Paleontologists have much evidence to convince them that this planet has been around for millions of years. The structure of the earth's surface and the fossil remains of its strata have all been used to teach that the days of creation necessitate geological ages of time. These viewpoints are consistently presented in textbooks used in high schools and colleges throughout the world.

The time needed for the development of the things in the order in which they are presented in Genesis 1. Of course, one approaches this particular point with a previous bias. Without the beliefs of evolution to confuse us, there is no reason why God could not have created things quickly in adult, mature, self-producing forms that reproduce "according to their own kind."

The interpretation of the phrase "evening and morning" as referring to "beginning and ending." This point is essential to the view that the days of creation are geological ages. Evidence for it is totally lacking in the biblical text. Whatever the phrase means, it is a key to the understanding of the word *day* in the creation account. If it only means "beginning and ending," then the possibility of the days being geological periods of time is greatly enhanced.

The events of Genesis 2 compared with Genesis 1:27. This particular argument is used by a great many "long-day" proponents. They view it as an insurmountable obstacle to the twenty-four-hour day view. Genesis 1:24-31 indicates that the sixth day of creation included the creation of living creatures on earth—cattle, creeping things, and beasts—as well as the man and the woman.

Genesis 2 records the details about the creation of the man and the woman, the planting of the garden, the placing of the man in the garden to tend and keep it, and the instruction about the trees in the garden. The very creation of woman required a "deep sleep" for Adam, all of which took too much time (according to this view) if it was all completed in a single twenty-four-hour day.

In spite of the simple logic of this view, it is not difficult to see all of these events occurring within one twenty-four-hour day. We are not talking about man's ability to achieve these things, but God's. He merely speaks the word, and it is done. No need for coffee breaks or long lunch hours to rest up a bit!

The evidence from church history. Josephus (a first century Jewish historian) expresses the long-day view of the creation account in Genesis, and so does Irenaeus, a church leader from the second century. Origen in the third century, Augustine in the fourth century, and Thomas Aquinas in the fourteenth century, all held the viewpoint that the days of creation were geological periods of time rather than twenty-four-hour days. Of course, a similar number of leaders could be cited who held that the days of creation were twenty-four-hour days.

The usage of the word "day." Proponents of the long-day view believe this is one of the most important arguments of all. They point out that Genesis 1:5 uses the Hebrew word *yom* to refer to a period of twelve hours, not twenty-four hours. The "light" was called "day" and the "darkness" was called "night."

Genesis 2:4 uses the singular "day " to refer to all the work God had done in creating the earth and the heavens. In this case, the word *day* refers to the six days of creation, regardless of how long they were individually.

It is quite true that the Bible uses the term *day* in various ways, but the great majority of its usages refer to a twenty-four-hour day. Is this a case where the word is used in a broader sense? We'll answer that shortly.

The usage of the Sabbath day. Those who hold the long-day theory of the days of creation frequently refer to the issue of the Sabbath day. According to Genesis 2:3, the seventh day was "blessed" and "sanctified" because God "rested from all His work" which He had done in creating the universe and all its life forms. But God continues to work. He sustains and preserves His created universe and continues to perform miraculous deeds. He has not stopped working. Jesus uses that point to justify His healing of a man on the Sabbath day. It was an act of mercy and fully allowable, though the Jewish leadership thought differently. Jesus clearly taught that the Father continues to work, even on a Sabbath day (John 5:1-17).

Adding to this argument, the long-day proponents refer to the teaching of Hebrews 4:1-10 as proof for their view. Hebrews 4:9 states, "There remains therefore a rest for the people of God." The obvious comparison of this passage with the day of God's rest, the seventh day of creation, and the implication that God's rest is still future and His works still continue, has led some to speak of the seventh day as continuing until our present day, thus indicating a long period of time.

However, the only thing from which God rested was His work of creating the heavens and the earth. It does not require that we eliminate God's activity which obviously has continued, nor does it require that we argue for a seventh day that has never ended.

God's perspective of time. A final argument often used by those who hold the long-day view of the days of creation is that of God's perspective of time. Days to Him are not limited to twenty-four hours. Peter tells us, "But, beloved, do not forget this one thing, that with the Lord one day is as a thousand years, and a thousand years as one day " (2 Peter 3:8; cf. Psalm 90:4).

It should be obvious that God does not view time as we do! However, that does not mean the days of creation are to be viewed similarly. If the biblical account is written from man's perspective and for his understanding, then this particular point would not be that significant.

**Reasons for the Days of Creation
Being Twenty-Four-Hour Days**

It is important to face immediately the implications of believing that the days of creation were twenty-four-hour days. It places its adherents in direct conflict with current scientific data and observation. It argues for a young earth thousands of years old rather than millions or billions of years old, even with "gaps" in the genealogical tables of the Bible.

The normal usage of the word "day." The Hebrew word *yom* and its plural form *yamim* are used over nineteen hundred times in the Bible. Out of all that usage, a mere sixty-five reveal a period of time other than a normal twenty-four-hour day.

The use of the numerical adjective. The numerical adjective is used two hundred times in the Bible with the Hebrew word *yom* (day), and seven hundred times with the plural form *yamim*. Whenever it is used, the word *day* refers to a twenty-four-hour day. Is Genesis chapter one an exception?

The phrase "evening and morning." We are told by proponents of the long-day view that this phrase simply means "beginning and ending." Where is the proof? In Daniel 8:14, Daniel was told the answer to his question about how long the temple and its sacrificial system would be trampled underfoot. The answer: "For two thousand three hundred days; then the sanctuary shall be cleansed." The word *days* in this verse is "evenings and mornings" in Hebrew, the same as Genesis chapter one.

The desecration of the sanctuary and its sacrificial system took place in the days of Antiochus Epiphanes in the second century before Christ. It lasted twenty-three hundred days. Then through the efforts of a Jewish revolt, inspired by Judas Maccabeus, the sanctuary was recaptured and cleansed. The desecration, prophesied by Daniel, lasted for over six years.

Those who argue that the phrase "evenings and mornings" in the book of Daniel likewise refers to a longer period of time speak of the twenty-three hundred days as twenty-three hundred years. They have decided that the "heavenly sanctuary" was cleansed around the nineteenth century by the blood of Jesus Christ, which was officially presented to the Father at that time for this cleansing to take place. Such reasoning is utter nonsense and, in fact, a violation of the New Testament teaching about the gospel.

Since the phrase in Daniel 8:14 must refer to normal twenty-four-hour days, it does present quite a case for the usage of the phrase "evening and morning" in Genesis 1 as also referring to twenty-four-hour days.

The relationship of the days of creation to the six-day work week. Exodus 20:8-11 records the fourth commandment of God given to Moses on Mount Sinai. It concerns the Sabbath day.

> Remember the Sabbath day, to keep it holy. Six days you shall labor and do all your work, but the seventh day is the sabbath of the LORD your God. In it you shall do no work: you, nor your son, nor your daughter, nor your manservant, nor your maidservant, nor your cattle, nor your stranger who is within your gates. For in six days the LORD made the heavens and the earth, the sea, and all that is in them, and rested the seventh day. Therefore the LORD blessed the Sabbath day and hallowed it.

Why is man required to work six days of the week and rest on the seventh day? Because "in six days the LORD made the heavens and the earth, the sea, and all that is in them, and rested the seventh day." That is a powerful argument for the days of creation being six twenty-four-hour days.

Those who believe the days are long periods of time argue that the point here is only one of comparison or analogy and not to be taken literally. They emphasize that the number of the days of the work week is based on the "six days" of creation, regardless of how long the days were.

The relationship of the Sabbath day. Advocates of the long-day theory of the days of creation use the Sabbath day to argue their point. God supposedly "rested" on the seventh day, yet He continues to work. They see the seventh day of creation as a day that continues for a long period of time, covering the history of man up until the present day.

Genesis 2:2-3 tells us that God "ended" His work of creation on the seventh day. He continues His work of preservation, sustaining the universe by His power and working actively in the affairs of humanity. But He "rested on the seventh day" from the work of creation.

There is no mention of the "sabbath day" in Genesis 2:2-3, but only the "seventh day." The Sabbath day is discussed in some detail in the Bible, and Exodus 31:13-17 describes its institution and the purpose for it. From that passage we learn the following:

1.   The Sabbath day instruction was given to the children of Israel.

2.   The Sabbath day is a sign between Israel and God, showing how they are "sanctified" (separated).

3.   The punishment for defiling the day is death.

4.   No work is to be done on that day.

5.   The Sabbath day is the seventh day of the week.

6.   The Sabbath day is to be practiced by the children of Israel forever.

7.   It is an everlasting reminder of the days of creation and, in particular, the seventh day, the day God rested from His work of creating.

The conclusion we must draw from this passage is that the seventh day of creation was the same as the normal Sabbath day of every normal week. The Sabbath day is a period of twenty-four hours, and it is based on the seventh day of creation, the day God ended His work of creating.

Summary of the Problem

If the days of creation are long periods of time (geological ages covering perhaps millions of years), then it is possible to reconcile "apparent" conflicts between the viewpoints of modern science concerning the age of the solar system and its various forms of life and the biblical account.

The difficulty arises when examining carefully the biblical account. One must constantly interpret the obvious in order to achieve the goal of reconciling scientific data with biblical statements. A simple reading of the Bible's statements leads one to believe that the six days of creation were normal twenty-four-hour days. If we were to believe that these days were geological ages, why would God not indicate such a view with more obvious statements rather than expressing it as it is? Why does it require so many explanations that seem interpretive and allegorical in order to prove the long-day view?

Perhaps we struggle too much. Is it not possible that the

available scientific data is wrong? Do we not hear continually of discoveries that make previously held scientific opinion clearly out-of-date and inaccurate? Is our effort to reconcile scientific data and theory with biblical statements a justifiable goal? Christianity believes in the supernatural, in miracles that are not acceptable to the scientific community. Do we believe in miracles, or can everything be explained by natural causes?

Christians begin with the assumption that the Bible *is* the Word of God, infallible, accurate in all its statements. We believe the accuracy and reliability of the Bible is guaranteed by God Himself, although human writers were used. We do not begin with scientific data. That has proven to be the wrong approach throughout the history of the church. If we allow scientific opinion to be the starting point of our investigation into truth, we will be greatly disappointed. Many of science's theories that have been contradictory to the Bible's teaching have in time proven to be false. Christians need to be patient.

The other side of this problem is that Christians should not discourage scientific investigation or believe that all scientists are atheists and hostile to Christianity. The available scientific data is important for all of us to study carefully. At times we will not be able to give an adequate answer or explanation. More time is needed. The truth is, many difficulties will not be resolved until we get to heaven. Our knowledge is so finite, limited by our own abilities and resources. We are not God, nor shall we ever be God!

If we must take sides, Christians should be patient and kind and continue to insist that though our interpretations of biblical statements are fallible and subject to error, the Bible's statements are accurate. We believe that additional information which can truly be described as fact will only confirm the validity and accuracy of the biblical account of creation.

Chapter 3

What Was Created in Six Days?

(1:3-25)

The majesty of the heavens, the beauty of the earth, the variety of animals, the uniqueness of humanity—did it all happen in six days? What about variation and mutation? Did all of the species known to us today begin during the six days of creation?

Exodus 20:11 states, "in six days the LORD made the heavens and the earth, the sea, and *all* (italics mine) that is in them." According to the Bible, it all began with the six days of creation, and everything that we see today and know to be in existence had its beginning when God created it all.

Day One
(1:3-5)

³Then God said, "Let there be light"; and there was light. ⁴And God saw the light, that it was good; and God divided the light from the darkness. ⁵God called the light Day, and the darkness He called Night. So the evening and the morning were the first day.

One of the interesting facts about the days of creation is the repetition of the phrase "Then God said." It appears in verses 3, 6, 9, 11, 14, 20, 24, 26, and 29, and begins the discussion of what happened on each creative day. On the third day it is stated twice, once for the gathering of the waters on the earth and once for the creation of plant life. On the sixth day it is stated twice, once for the creation of beasts, cattle, and creeping things and once for the creation of man and woman.

The clear implication of what the Bible says about each day of creation is that all that takes place is the result of the spoken word of God. Nothing more is needed, no further explanations are given. When God says it, it happens. From this simple truth, we would have to question all viewpoints that demand geological ages to complete what God simply stated would happen. How long does it take for the word of God to accomplish these things?

According to Genesis 1:2, "darkness was on the face of the deep." On the first day of creation, it does not specifically state that God spoke the darkness into being. He merely called the darkness "night." What came into existence by the spoken word of God was light.

The activity of God on day one includes:

1. What God said—"let there be light."

2. What God saw—"the light, that it was good."

3. What God divided—"the light from the darkness."

4. What God called—"the light Day . . . the darkness . . . Night."

Creation is the work of God, operating alone and independently of outside forces or resources.

It is not necessary to demand the presence of the sun, moon, and stars on day one in order to insure the statements about light and darkness. (Many have jumped to the conclusion that the sun, moon, and stars are included in the opening statement of Genesis 1 ("the heavens"), and that day four was not the creation of these stellar entities but that they merely appeared on that day. More about that later when we come to day four.) Revelation 21:23 speaks of the heavenly city called New Jerusalem and says: "And the city had no need of the sun or of the moon to shine in it, for the glory of God illuminated it, and the Lamb is its light." The only light that is needed is that which comes from God Himself! If that is true in our eternal state, why is it not possible on the first day of creation?

The importance of God creating the light is emphasized by the apostle Paul in 2 Corinthians 4:6: "For it is the God who commanded light to shine out of darkness who has shone in our hearts to give the light of the knowledge of the glory of God in the face of Jesus Christ." The ability to become a Christian is based upon the power of God to "turn the lights on," so to speak. The same God Who spoke the light into existence can do the same in the human heart.

Day Two
(1:6-8)

⁶Then God said, "Let there be a firmament in the midst of the waters, and let it divide the waters from the waters." ⁷Thus God made the firmament, and divided the waters which were under the firmament from the waters which were above the firmament; and it was so. ⁸And God called the firmament Heaven. So the evening and the morning were the second day.

The second day of creation begins the same as day one—"Then God said." Once you start with the spoken word of God, it is a simple step to see how things were created without previously existing material (Hebrews 11:3). Faith expresses total confidence in what God says.

The formula of God's activity on day two is "God said, God made, God divided, and God called." The issue is "a firmament"; God will call it Heaven. Some have confused this firmament called Heaven with the sun, moon, and stars. But if we read the biblical account carefully, we will notice from Genesis 1:17 that "God set [the sun, moon, and stars] in the firmament of the heavens." The firmament was in existence before the sun, moon, and stars were placed in it.

Psalm 19:1 says "the firmament shows His handiwork." Psalm 150:1 tells us to "Praise Him in His mighty firmament!" And Daniel 12:3 says, "Those who are wise shall shine / Like the brightness of the firmament."

I like to refer to the firmament as "outer space." But because it was created by God, it cannot be infinite as God Himself. The created is limited by the Creator, and though the extent of that which He created is not observable by us, it nevertheless, out of necessity, must have limitations. God knows how extensive is the expanse which He Himself created.

Some believe the firmament only refers to the earth's atmosphere. This, they believe, is required by the statement that God "divided the waters which were under the firmament from the waters which were above the firmament." The "waters under the firmament" are, no doubt, the waters of Genesis 1:2, and refer to the waters of planet earth. This is clear from the activity of day three where God gathers these waters into one place and calls them "seas."

Some believe the "waters above the firmament" refer to a vapor canopy that existed in pre-flood days, creating a tropical greenhouse effect for the beautiful environment of the planet. Those who hold to this view believe that the vapor canopy collapsed at the time of the flood, explaining the tremendous volume of water that was dumped on the earth. They would see the statement of Genesis 7:11, "and the windows of heaven were opened," as proof of this view concerning the "waters above the firmament."

There is no way to prove this. The volume of water necessary for the universal flood of Genesis does not need to come from a torrential rainfall. These issues will be discussed in some detail when we come to the account of the flood.

Perhaps the "waters above the firmament" are the same as a later reference to "waters above the heavens," which is likely a reference to the rain God brings (Psalm 148:4, 104:13). But before the rain ever came upon the planet, God placed "waters above the firmament." What is meant by this, we cannot say with certainty. Bible believers, however, remain confident of this one fact—there are "waters above the firmament"!

The term "heaven" needs a bit of explanation. According to Genesis 1:1, "God created the heavens." More than one. The firmament or expanse of outer space is called "heaven," not "heavens." Yet in Genesis 1:17 God speaks of the "firmament of the heavens."

The earth's atmosphere is called "heaven" in the Bible. Outer space with its millions of stars is also described as "heaven." The place where God dwells is described as "heaven." The heavenly city called "the New Jerusalem" comes out of "heaven" where God's throne is. Paul refers to the "third heaven" in 2 Corinthians 12:2, calling it "Paradise (v. 4)." From his words, we assume that there are at least three heavens.

After examining the usage of the word "heaven" and the plural "heavens," it seems that we should not be too dogmatic about these terms. One fact is clear: Whatever "heavens" are, they were created by God. The "heaven" that includes the sun, moon, and stars was created by God on day two, and God divided on that day the waters that were under the firmament from the waters above it.

Day Three
(1:9-13)

⁹**Then God said, "Let the waters under the heavens be gathered together into one place, and let the dry land appear"; and it was so. ¹⁰And God called the dry land Earth, and the gathering together of the waters He called Seas. And God saw that it was good. ¹¹Then God said, "Let the earth bring forth grass, the herb that yields seed, and the fruit tree that yields fruit according to its kind, whose seed is in itself, on the earth"; and it was so. ¹²And the earth brought forth grass, the herb that yields seed according to its kind, and the tree that yields fruit, whose seed is in itself according to its kind. And God saw that it was good. ¹³So the evening and the morning were the third day.**

God spoke twice on this third day. He first spoke the words that caused the waters of the earth to gather into designated areas, resulting in the appearance of dry land. He next spoke the words that brought plant life into existence.

The general theory of evolution is clearly incompatible with a literal interpretation of the days of creation. Day three presents an enormous problem—the creation of plant life before the sun on day four or marine organisms on day five. Evolutionists cannot imagine the survival of vegetation without the sun. They also hold that trees evolved from marine organisms.

Dry land was not created on day three. The text says "let the dry land appear." Land was not visible before day three. The earth was covered with water (Genesis 1:2). On day three, God gathered the waters together to form what He called Seas. A fascinating look at this third day of creation is provided by the psalmist in Psalm 104:5-13:

> You who laid the foundations of the earth,
> So that it should not be moved forever,
> You covered it with the deep as with a garment;
> The waters stood above the mountains.
> At Your rebuke they fled;
> At the voice of Your thunder they hastened away.
> They went up over the mountains;
> They went down into the valleys,
> To the place which You founded for them.

41

You have set a boundary that they may not pass over,
That they may not return to cover the earth.
He sends the springs into the valleys,
Which flow among the hills.
They give drink to every beast of the field;
The wild donkeys quench their thirst.
By them the birds of the heavens have their habitation;
They sing among the branches.
He waters the hills from His upper chambers;
The earth is satisfied with the fruit of Your works.

These verses indicate that the earth, including its mountain ranges, was covered with water when God began His creation. At the sound of His voice, the waters receded into "the place" which God had "founded for them." These oceanic caverns contain the water necessary to cover the entire globe, extending above the mountains. These verses suggest that the water necessary to cause a universal flood is presently residing in the depths of the earth, a fascinating fact as it relates to the biblical account of the flood.

On that very same day, God said the words that brought plant life into existence. The planet had been literally soaking in water until this day began. There was enough moisture to sustain the plants that God would place upon the dry land. There was light (from the first day), even though the sun, moon, and stars did not come into existence until the fourth day.

Genesis 1:11 states that God ordered the earth to "bring forth" its plant life. The earth is granted power to sprout grass, herbs, and fruit trees. We learn three amazing facts about the creation of plant life from these verses: (1) The trees were capable of yielding fruit; (2) the seed was already in the fruit of the trees; and (3) these plants were reproducing according to their own kind.

This presentation is in total disagreement with the process and viewpoints of evolution. Evolutionists would complain on at least four levels:

1. Plants cannot survive without sunlight, which does not come until the fourth day.

2. Plants and trees evolved from marine organisms, which do not come until the fifth day.

3. Plants cannot begin as self-producing biological units containing their own seeds.

4. Reproduction is not restricted to categories described as "kinds."

The phrase "according to its kind" or "after its kind" has generated a great deal of discussion and debate. The phrase is used of fish, birds, beasts, cattle, and creeping things on the earth. They all reproduce "according to its kind." The Hebrew word for kind, *min*, is used thirty-one times by Moses, the author of the first five books of the Bible. (See Leviticus 11 for examples of how *kind* is used.)

Current classifications of animal life include about one million species. Whether the word *species* is the same as our biblical word *kind*, we simply do not know. The biblical term probably refers to a smaller set of classifications than species.

Whatever the meaning of *kind*, it will not change its essential character. While mutation or variation might occur, the essential kind will not change or reproduce differently. This, of course, contradicts the theory of evolution. There are essential differences in the animal world that can never be changed. Fish cannot become birds, birds cannot become reptiles, and so on.

Day Four
(1:14-19)

¹⁴Then God said, "Let there be lights in the firmament of the heavens to divide the day from the night; and let them be for signs and seasons, and for days and years; ¹⁵and let them be for lights in the firmament of the heavens to give light on the earth"; and it was so. ¹⁶Then God made two great lights: the greater light to rule the day, and the lesser light to rule the night. He made the stars also. ¹⁷God set them in the firmament of the heavens to give light on the earth, ¹⁸and to rule over the day and over the night, and to divide the light from the darkness. And God saw that it was good. ¹⁹So the evening and the morning were the fourth day.

The order of God's activity on the fourth day of creation is "God said, God made, God set, and God saw." The issues of the fourth day are crucial to the whole argument of creation versus evolution.

There is no evidence from these verses that the sun and stars merely "appeared" on the fourth day. While that viewpoint is held by many theologians and scientists, the biblical record does not support it. When God wanted to reveal that something merely appeared that He had previously created, He made it quite clear. Genesis 1:9 states that the dry land appeared. The earth was created previously but was covered with water. When the waters were gathered together on the third day of creation, the dry land appeared.

The word *appear* is not used on the fourth day in relation to the sun, moon, and stars. The language employed is that used on the previous days of creation. God speaks and says "Let there be lights in the firmament of the heavens." That assumes that they were not in existence previously. Genesis 1:16 is clear when it states, "God *made* two great lights . . . the stars also." The word *made* is used interchangeably with the word *create*.

Genesis 1:17 adds an additional point to the fact that the sun, moon, and stars were created on the fourth day, rather than merely being made to appear. It says that "God set them in the firmament of the heavens." That implies that they were not there previously.

The Jewish source, Meam Loez, makes this interesting observation about the fourth day:

> The sun was created after the earth to dispel any notion that the creation of earth was a natural result of the sun's heat vaporizing the waters. Similarly, lest anyone contend that plant-life is a natural outgrowth of the earth (aided by the sun), God created the earth and all its properties on the third day, and only afterwards, on the fourth day, did He create the sun, to demonstrate unequivocally that everything materialized from God's direct will. (*Bereishis*, vol. 1, translation and commentary by Rabbi Meir Zlotowitz, (New York: Mesorah Publications Ltd., 1977), p. 59)

What Is the Purpose of the Sun, Moon, and Stars?

Physical purposes.

1. To give light on the earth. Genesis 1:15 states that these lights are "to give light on the earth." This fact is repeated in verse 17. Psalm 148:1 exhorts us to "Praise the LORD," and then calls upon all His creation to praise Him. Verse 3 says "Praise Him, sun and moon; Praise Him, all you stars of light!" The purpose of these celestial bodies is to give light upon the earth. These light sources are not to be worshiped by the inhabitants of earth. We are not their servants—they are to serve us.

2. To divide the day from the night, the light from the darkness. Verse 14 says that God spoke these lights into existence in order "to divide the day from the night." Verse 18 adds, "to divide the light from the darkness." Instead of night and day depending upon the original light source of day one, the light-dark sequence of planet earth is now dependent upon the sun, moon, and stars. Of course, the rotation of the earth in relation to the sun affects this issue.

3. To rule over the day and the night. The concept of ruling over the affairs of the earth (v. 16) may include the issue of time and how to calculate it. Verse 14 says that these lights are designed to set the pattern "for days and years." Before our present dating system was established, every calendar of ancient peoples was based on changes observed in the moon. This lunar system of dating was rooted in God's original purpose.

Psalm 136:7-9 confirms the original creation account:

> To Him who made great lights,
> For His mercy endures forever—
> The sun to rule by day,
> For His mercy endures forever;
> The moon and stars to rule by night,
> For His mercy endures forever.

Spiritual purposes. In Genesis 1:14 we read that God designed the sun, moon, and stars "for signs and seasons." The Bible indicates several symbolic purposes for the creation of these celestial bodies.

1. To demonstrate God's faithfulness. Psalm 89:33-37 records this remarkable purpose of God:

> Nevertheless My lovingkindness I will not utterly take
>   from him,
> Nor allow My faithfulness to fail.
> My covenant I will not break,
> Nor alter the word that has gone out of My lips.
> Once I have sworn by My holiness;

> I will not lie to David:
> His seed shall endure forever, And his throne as the
> sun before Me;
> It shall be established forever like the moon,
> Even like the faithful witness in the sky.

God's promises for the survival and future glory of the nation of Israel are based upon the "faithful witness in the sky." God's promise that the descendants of King David will endure forever is connected to the "ordinances" of sun, moon, and stars (Jeremiah 31:35-36).

2. To demonstrate God's power. God sustains the stars, calls them all by name, and has created them all—what mighty power (Psalm 147:4-5, Isaiah 40:25-26)! When the psalmist looked into the heavens, he could not help reflecting on God's concern for humanity:

> When I consider Your heavens, the work of Your
> fingers,
> The moon and the stars, which You have ordained,
> What is man that You are mindful of him,
> And the son of man that You visit him?
>
> (Psalm 8:3-4)

It is indeed incredible that the God Who made the sun, moon, and stars has deep and personal concern for people!

3. To demonstrate God's coming judgment. The prophet Joel spoke of the day when there would be wonders (signs) in the heavens (2:30-31). The sun would be turned into darkness and the moon into blood "before the coming of the great and terrible day of the LORD." The Gospels also speak of a coming day of judgment when "the sun will be darkened, and the moon will not give its light; the stars will fall from heaven, and the powers of the heavens will be shaken" (Matthew 24:29; cf. Luke 21:25-28). These unusual events in the sun, moon, and stars point to God's coming judgment.

4. To demonstrate God's purpose. Genesis 1:14 speaks of the sun, moon, and stars as being designed by God "for seasons." The Hebrew word is used over two hundred times in the Bible, and over half of these usages occur in the context of a gathering for worship. The word *seasons* points to celebration, feasts, and worship. In fact, the religious calendar of the Jewish people is based on the visual changes in the moon. The "seasons" in

Genesis 1:14 are designed to fulfill God's purpose for His people; He wants us to worship Him.

The first four days of creation describe the wonder of God's character and provision for humanity. What a delight to see His power and purposes being fulfilled! His attributes are being displayed, and all that He does in creation should cause us to give Him praise.

Day Five
(1:20-23)

²⁰Then God said, "Let the waters abound with an abundance of living creatures, and let birds fly above the earth across the face of the firmament of the heavens." ²¹So God created great sea creatures and every living thing that moves, with which the waters abounded, according to their kind, and every winged bird according to its kind. And God saw that it was good. ²²And God blessed them, saying, "Be fruitful and multiply, and fill the waters in the seas, and let birds multiply on the earth." ²³So the evening and the morning were the fifth day.

The statements of God's activity on the fifth day are "God said, God created, God saw, and God blessed." The Hebrew word *bārā'* is used for the second time in the creation account. The first occasion was the opening verse, "In the beginning God created." The next occasion will be Genesis 1:27 where we read, "So God created man . . . male and female He created them." The word "create" and the word "made" are used interchangeably (see Genesis 2:3), and thus a great deal of importance should not be placed upon the actual occurrences of the word "create" as though its usages are the only evidence of God's creative work. All that occurs during the six days speaks of His creative power.

What about Fish?

God's words indicate that the waters of the earth were to be filled with fish of all kinds. The text says "let the waters abound with an abundance of living creatures." God commands them to "be fruitful and multiply and fill the waters in the seas," the same message He gives to man and woman in Genesis 1:28.

Verse 21 counters the arguments of evolution regarding marine organisms; these creatures of the sea were reproducing "according to their kind." Whatever their kind, they did not alter their makeup through reproduction. God fixed the uniqueness of these kinds and never implies that they evolved into some "higher" order of animal life.

Psalm 104:24-26 is a wonderful commentary on God's creation of fish and various creatures of the sea:

> O LORD, how manifold are Your works!
> In wisdom You have made them all.
> The earth is full of Your possessions—
> This great and wide sea,
> In which are innumerable teeming things,
> Living things both small and great.
> There the ships sail about;
> And there is that Leviathan
> Which You have made to play there.

God's wisdom is displayed in the fish He created. They reveal the variety of His creative work—all kinds of animals in the sea, all proclaiming the unique wisdom of God.

What Is Leviathan?

Psalm 104:26 speaks of a great sea creature which God made and calls it "Leviathan." Job 41 refers to this creature and says that "on earth there is nothing like him" (v. 33). This sea animal is presented as an impossible creature for man to conquer or catch. Since God made it, it demonstrates how great God's power is. This is God's answer to Job about all his troubles and concerns regarding the purposes and power of God. Just take a look at Leviathan! According to Job 42:1-6, the message spoke to Job's heart, and he responded as God desired and subsequently was blessed richly by the Lord.

The account in Job 41 presents a creature of incredible size and power. This sea creature cannot be conquered by "harpoons" or "fishing spears" (v. 7). It has "scales" that seem impossible to remove (vv. 15-17). This creature has "sparks of fire" shooting out of its mouth and "smoke goes out of his nostrils" (vv. 19-20). A sword, spear, dart, or javelin is helpless against this creature (v. 26), and it apparently is an awesome sight when it stands up (v. 25). The water in which he plays seems like a boiling pot.

Is this a description of a dinosaur? An article in the January 1982 issue of *Scientific American* magazine examines different explanations for what is called "the mysterious disappearance" of dinosaurs from the earth at the end of the Mesozoic era, some sixty-three million years ago. The article explains that "the disappearances were the result of a catastrophic disruption of the biosphere by an extraterrestrial agency." In other words, we don't know why the dinosaurs disappeared!

It is standard procedure to argue that people as we know them today were not in existence when these extremely large creatures were roaming the earth. The scientific evidence, however, is inconclusive.

If dinosaurs did roam the earth at the same time as humans, where did they come from? The Bible seems to imply that God created them. It is very possible that the Leviathan of Job 41 and Psalm 104 is something like the plesiosaur.

In the book of Job we are introduced to another incredible animal called "Behemoth." When the Lord gave His final answer to Job, He brought to Job's attention two animals that were so powerful, Job (or anyone else!) could not handle them. The Lord's point is that He made them, and therefore, these large animals (known to Job) should remind Job of the Lord's power.

Behemoth "eats grass like an ox" (Job 40:15) and has a giant tail and a body structure that seems invincible (vv. 16-18). This animal is called "the first of the ways of God," a possible reminder of the days of creation. Verse 19 continues, "Only He who made him can bring near His sword." God is the only one who can handle this beast. It is possible that this description is that of a brontosaurus.

There are several scholars who argue that Behemoth is a hippopotamus and Leviathan is a giant alligator or crocodile. The language of Job 40-41 does not reveal that clearly. It seems more likely that animal creatures of greater size and power are demanded by the passage. Naturally, it is of great concern to those who believe that humans did not live at the time of the dinosaurs. Those who say that dinosaurs were extinct sixty-three million years ago would, of course, not believe that Job was living while they were still around.

What happened to the dinosaurs? It is very possible that these large creatures were destroyed suddenly at the time of the Genesis flood, thus explaining their fossil remains in the strata of earth's surface. The large mammoths discovered in the ice of

Siberia had tropical vegetation in their mouths.

What about Birds?

The fifth day produced an abundance of marine life and also filled the sky with birds. Genesis 1:20 says "let birds fly above the earth across the face of the firmament of the heavens." Verse 22 says "let birds multiply on the earth," and verse 21 states that God created "every winged bird according to its kind." God gave individual attention to each "kind," and in the marvelous variety which we now observe in the bird kingdom, we see the touch of our God.

When Jesus Christ was teaching us about trusting the Lord and not worrying about basic needs, He drew our attention to the birds: "Look at the birds of the air, for they neither sow nor reap nor gather into barns; yet your heavenly Father feeds them. Are you not of more value than they?" (Matthew 6:26). God made the birds to teach us lessons about our value and our need to trust the One Who made us and has promised to take care of us.

Day Six
(1:24-25)

²⁴**Then God said, "Let the earth bring forth the living creature according to its kind: cattle and creeping thing and beast of the earth, each according to its kind"; and it was so. ²⁵And God made the beast of the earth according to its kind, cattle according to its kind, and everything that creeps on the earth according to its kind. And God saw that it was good.**

On this day two major events occur: the creation of land animals, and the creation of man and woman. What an amazing day the sixth day was! It was the final day of God's creative work. (We'll look at His creation of the land animals here, and devote the entire next chapter to a discussion of His creation of man and woman.)

God's activity is described as "God said, God made, God saw." He speaks, He acts, He observes. These three activities of God, in a special way, summarize His activity on our behalf.

When God created the land animals on the sixth day, the biblical record emphasizes three categories: (1) the beast of the earth; (2) the cattle; and (3) everything that creeps on the earth. All three of these categories are described in verse 24 as "the living creature." When the biblical text uses the words "let the earth bring forth," some scholars believe that this implies that God is using previously existing material in order to create the land animals. That is possible but certainly not necessary.

These animals are said to have "living souls." Like the fish and birds (vv. 20-21), they have a life similar to humans, though they are not described as being made in God's image and after His likeness.

The "beast" created on the sixth day is distinct from the "cattle." Some believe the distinctions deal with diet as well as the issue of control. The beast is wild and uncontrolled whereas the cattle are domesticated. Most commentators believe the term "cattle" refers to those animals which serve man's needs (ox, donkey, mule, horse, camel, sheep, cow). Some say the term refers to grass-eating animals. The "beasts of the earth" seem to refer to wildlife, such as the lion, wolf, bear, panther, and tiger.

The phrase "everything that creeps on the earth" probably refers to creatures that move without feet or with feet that one can hardly see. It refers to worms, insects, and reptiles. Leviticus 11:20-23 lists a few of those insects that "creep" on the earth.

The animals were intended by God to be lessons to humanity about His purposes and plans for us. Proverbs 6:6-11 exhorts us by appealing to the industry and ways of the ant. Proverbs 30:18-31 uses various animals to teach us and reveal to us the wisdom of God. Psalm 104 speaks of the marvelous care of God for the animals He created. Consider a few of the blessings He intended for them (vv. 10-30):

> He sends the springs into the valleys,
> . . . .
> They give drink to every beast of the field.
>
> He causes the grass to grow for the cattle.
>
> The trees of the LORD are full of sap,
> . . . .
> Where the birds make their nests;
> The stork has her home in the fir trees.
> The high hills are for the wild goats;
> The cliffs are a refuge for the rock badgers.
>
> The young lions roar after their prey,
> And seek their food from God.

> This great and wide sea,
> In which are innumerable teeming things
> ·
> Which You have made to play there.
> These all wait for You,
> That You may give them their food in due season.

> You open Your hand, they are filled with good.

All of God's animals are designed to speak of His glory and power and to praise His name. Psalm 148:7, 10 says:

> Praise the LORD from the earth,
> You great sea creatures and all the depths;
> ·
> Beasts and all cattle;
> Creeping things and flying fowl.

According to the Bible, everything that God has made is to praise Him. That includes you and me. A person can go all his or her life making plans, conducting business, setting goals, trying to survive, and miss the ultimate meaning and purpose of it all. God made you for Himself. The Creator asks the created to honor, praise, worship, adore, give thanks, and glorify Him in everything.

How do you and I measure up?

Chapter 4
The Creation of Human Life
(1:26-31)

Human life is at the heart of our difficulties with a study of origins. Where did we come from, why are we here, and where are we going? These are the basic questions from which the business of life, health, happiness, and the future finds meaning and value.

This generation is confused about values, ethics, and the meaning and purpose of life itself. One reason for our mental and emotional confusion is the failure to understand the origin of human life. Were we created by God and thus accountable to Him, or are we the product of evolutionary process, mere examples of animals who have achieved a high level of intelligence and productivity?

It is at this point that the greatest hostility and opposition is experienced between the teachings of modern science and those of Christianity. The Christian view is ridiculed frequently in the classroom, while the doctrines of evolution are accepted without question. Is this just a religious issue? Are theologians ignorant of scientific discovery or too stubborn to admit that their views are not reliable in the light of scientific "fact"?

What the Bible Says about the Origin of Human Life
(1:26-31)

²⁶Then God said, "Let Us make man in Our image, according to Our likeness; let them have dominion over the fish of the sea, over the birds of the air, and over the cattle, over all the earth and over every creeping thing that creeps on the earth." ²⁷So God

**created man in His own image; in the image of God
He created him; male and female He created them.
²⁸Then God blessed them, and God said to them, "Be
fruitful and multiply; fill the earth and subdue it; have
dominion over the fish of the sea, over the birds of
the air, and over every living thing that moves on the
earth."**

**²⁹And God said, "See, I have given you every herb that
yields seed which is on the face of all the earth, and
every tree whose fruit yields seed; to you it shall be for
food. ³⁰Also, to every beast of the earth, to every bird
of the air, and to everything that creeps on the earth, in
which there is life, I have given every green herb for
food"; and it was so. ³¹Then God saw everything that He
had made, and indeed it was very good. So the evening
and the morning were the sixth day.**

The words "Then God said" and "So God created" clearly
teach that human life is the result of the creative work of God.
Genesis 2:7 indicates that man becomes "a living being" because
of the "breath of life" being placed directly into him from God
alone. A parallel expression occurs in the book of Job:

The Spirit of God has made me,
And the breath of the Almighty gives me life.
. . . .
If He should gather to Himself His Spirit and His
breath,
All flesh would perish together,
And man would return to dust.

(33:4, 34:14-15)

In the New Testament, James tells us: "For as the body
without the spirit is dead, so faith without works is dead also"
(2:26). Life comes from the presence of the spirit within the
physical body. This life is the result of the "breath of God"
Himself.

The Bible teaches that when an individual becomes a
Christian he is a "new creation" (2 Corinthians 5:17). The Bible
calls the experience of becoming a Christian an act of creation:
"we are His workmanship, created in Christ Jesus" (Ephesians
2:10), and Ephesians 4:24 speaks of "the new man which was
created according to God, in righteousness and true holiness."

Life is more than physically surviving; it involves our spiritual nature, our capacity and ability to know the God Who made us and to relate to Him personally.

Where Did Our Bodies Come From?

When a person asks about the origin of the physical body the Bible makes it clear that it was designed by God out of the dust of the ground (Genesis 2:7). Genesis 3:19 adds that when physical death occurs, the body will return to the dust of the ground.

> In the sweat of your face you shall eat bread
> Till you return to the ground,
> For out of it you were taken;
> For dust you are,
> And to dust you shall return.

When people die, the body (if not cremated) will decay; it will become dust and prove the accuracy of biblical statements.

Psalm 103:13-18 speaks of God's compassion in the light of the transitory nature of physical life:

> As a father pities his children,
> So the LORD pities those who fear Him.
> For he knows our frame;
> He remembers that we are dust.

> As for man, his days are like grass;
> As a flower of the field, so he flourishes.
> For the wind passes over it, and it is gone,
> And its place remembers it no more.
> But the mercy of the LORD is from everlasting to
> everlasting
> On those who fear Him,
> And His righteousness to children's children,
> To such as keep His covenant,
> And to those who remember His commandments to
> do them.

The Bible is clear—the material part of human life, the physical body, was made by God out of the dust of the ground. God knows that fact better than any one of us. Because He knows the truth about our physical bodies, He has great compassion and love for us. What a wonderful insight!

How Valuable Are We?

Questions of worth and self-esteem are powerful issues in our culture. We struggle with them often because we leave God out of the picture. We pretend that it does not matter whether we were created in His image or not.

Yet self-esteem is rooted in the act of creation. Understanding this truth can set us free. The simple statement of Genesis 1:26-27 that we were created puts value upon us. That act of creation produced creatures that have the "image of God" and the "likeness of God." We are not God, but there is much about us that is like Him. He thinks, and so do we; He feels deeply, and our emotions are obvious; He makes decisions and exercises His will, and so do we. We are aware of the fact that we exist and have the mental capacity to project into the future, to plan ahead, to evaluate the past in the light of the present—these marks of human personality are rooted in the nature of God Himself.

James 3:8-10 warns against the evil of degrading other human beings by our words:

> But no man can tame the tongue. It is an unruly evil, full of deadly poison. With it we bless our God and Father, and with it we curse men, who have been made in the similitude [likeness] of God. Out of the same mouth proceed blessing and cursing. My brethren, these things ought not to be so.

We have no right to curse other human beings for we have all been made in the likeness of God. Our worth is based on the creation of God; we are valuable because we have been made in His image and after His likeness.

The whole issue of the sanctity of life is rooted in the creation as well. Immediately after the flood, God instructs Noah about capital punishment for capital crime (Genesis 9:6):

> Whoever sheds man's blood,
> By man his blood shall be shed;
> For in the image of God
> He made man.

Why should society not tolerate premeditated murder? Why should the individual who murders be put to death? Because God is cruel, because such treatment is barbaric? No way!

Murderers should be put to death because human beings are valuable to God, and no one has the right to take another person's life without due process of law and undeniable conviction of a murderous act. Because we were made in the image of God, human life is precious. No one has the right to destroy it by murder and senseless killing.

The special worth of humanity is determined by four things in Genesis 1:26-31.

Our personality—we were made "in the image of God."

Our position over the animal world—we were told to "have dominion over" all the fish, birds, cattle, and creeping things. Psalm 8:3-8 speaks of humanity's dominion over the animal world, thus establishing the special worth of mankind:

> When I consider Your heavens, the work of Your
>   fingers,
> The moon and the stars, which You have ordained,
> What is man that You are mindful of him,
> And the son of man that You visit him?
> For You have made him a little lower than the angels,
>   And You have crowned him with glory and
>   honor.
>
> You have made him to have dominion over the works
>   of Your hands;
> You have put all things under his feet,
> All sheep and oxen—
> Even the beasts of the field,
> The birds of the air,
> And the fish of the sea
> That pass through the paths of the seas.

Obviously, human beings are of much greater value than the animals which God also created. Self-worth and value are rooted in the origins of human life.

The provision of our physical needs—"to you it shall be for food" (v. 29). The words of Genesis 1:29-30 indicate that the diet of human beings was designed to be distinct from that of the animals.

²⁹And God said, "See, I have given you every herb that yields seed which is on the face of all the earth,

and every tree whose fruit yields seed; to you it shall be for food. ³⁰Also, to every beast of the earth, to every bird of the air, and to everything that creeps on the earth, in which there is life, I have given every green herb for food"; and it was so.

Trees without fruit could be used for lumber and fuel, but the fruit trees were uniquely designed by God to provide food for the physical needs of humanity. The animals can eat "every green herb," a diet of plants and vegetation, but human beings need the "herb that yields seed" and the "fruit" of trees "whose fruit yields seed."

The plan of God to propagate the human race—"be fruitful and multiply; fill the earth." The value of life is determined not only by the fact that we were made in the image of God, given dominion over the animal world, and provided a special and unique diet, distinct from the animals, but we also have special worth because of God's plan to propagate the human race.

Consider carefully these words from Genesis 1:28:

Then God blessed them, and God said to them, "Be fruitful and multiply; fill the earth and subdue it; have dominion over the fish of the sea, over the birds of the air, and over every living thing that moves on the earth."

God's plan to propagate the race is described as a "blessing"— God "blessed them." Out of the 613 commandments of God's law, this is usually stated to be the first commandment He gave to the human race. But is it a command or is it a blessing? We believe it is both.

God wants us to have children, and He tells us that we are being blessed, not punished, when we do so. Psalm 127:3-5 gives us some additional information about the blessing of children:

Behold, children are a heritage from the LORD,
The fruit of the womb is His reward.
Like arrows in the hand of a warrior,
So are the children of one's youth.
Happy is the man who has his quiver full of them;
They shall not be ashamed,
But shall speak with their enemies in the gate.

The Bible says a person is happy who has lots of children! Psalm

128:1-6 includes children as a part of God's blessing to the people of Israel, the reward of their obedience to Him.

Today's culture has decided that children are a problem and can keep a young married couple from enjoying themselves. The age of bearing children is becoming much older than previous generations. The idea of a couple having double incomes with no children is very popular. God's standards of blessing have not changed. He wants us to have children.

The worth of humanity is clearly seen not only in the plan of God to propagate the race, but in the fact that this command and blessing is immediately connected to the dominion of man and woman over the animal world. Human beings are the highest order of life which God Himself created!

A Final Summary

In summarizing all that took place during those six days of creation, we have these words in Genesis 1:31:

Then God saw everything that He had made, and indeed it was very good. So the evening and the morning were the sixth day.

Not just "good," but "very good"! That was the evaluation of God Himself. It was a delight to the heart of God to see the universe, the sun, moon, and stars, the plants and trees, the fish and birds, the animals of all kinds, and of course, the man and woman, Adam and Eve. What a wonderful world it must have been! A paradise indeed—"very good"!

The world has been cluttered by man's inventions and decisions. The good blessings of God have been polluted and defiled. Our world, from an ecological and environmental point of view, is in dire straits. Many couldn't care less. Most hope and pray that our scientists will solve our problems and allow "the good life" to continue with all its modern conveniences.

Many of us have forsaken interest in the God of creation, choosing rather to adopt the viewpoints of evolutionary thinking. Are we just highly developed animals? Does the God of the Bible really exist? Are we accountable to Him? Is our self-worth and esteem rooted in the facts of creation or in the circumstances of our lives?

The questions continue. Without God, they remain unsolved.

Chapter 5
The Seventh Day
(2:1-3)

Saturday, the seventh day of the week, is a traditional day of rest. Many businesses organize themselves around a Monday-to Friday schedule, leaving Saturday and Sunday for the discretion of the employee. Beliefs about the day and its importance abound in many religions of the world. Islam observes Friday as its sacred day of worship and rest. The majority of Christians choose Sunday as the special day for religious observance. Jewish people (and a number of Christians) observe Saturday as the special day for worship and rest.

It all starts with what the Bible teaches in Genesis 2:1-3 about the seventh day of the week.

> **¹Thus the heavens and the earth, and all the host of them, were finished. ²And on the seventh day God ended His work which He had done, and He rested on the seventh day from all His work which He had done. ³Then God blessed the seventh day and sanctified it, because in it He rested from all His work which God had created and made.**

When I was a young boy, growing up in a Christian home, my parents believed that this seventh day was "blessed and sanctified" by God and that Christians honored it by going to church on Sunday and by doing nothing worldly or strenuous on that day. I can remember being mildly rebuked for asking, "Why do we do this on Sunday, since Saturday is the seventh day?" Little boys were to be seen, not heard. (Especially me—I could ask more questions than any person could answer!)

We never mowed the lawn or went to the store on Sunday. We went to church in the morning (the sermon often went until 1:00 P.M.) and again at night. In the afternoon we were told to rest. The one thing I was allowed to do was to read the Sunday newspaper, although the comic section was considered too worldly.

How things have changed in a single generation! Sunday "blue laws" (laws against businesses operating on Sunday) have been dropped, and people do most anything on Sundays these days, even when they express commitment to the beliefs of Christianity.

Jewish people (and some Christians) refer to Saturday as the Sabbath, a Hebrew word for "rest," appearing over a hundred times in the Old Testament and sixty-eight times in the New. Saturday is the Sabbath, no matter what your religious belief. The problem is that some Christians in church history spoke of Sunday as "the Christian Sabbath," perhaps a reaction to Jewish beliefs about the day. Regardless of your particular religious background, Saturday is the Sabbath. It has never been any other day of the week.

All of this discussion (and argument!) among religious groups has one original source—the Bible's teaching about the sanctity and specialness of the seventh day.

The Seventh Day was Declared by God to Be the Day He Ended His Work of Creation

Genesis 2:2 begins with these words "on the seventh day God ended His work." From this it might appear that God's work of creation continued until the seventh day and did not cease until that day had already begun. However, the preposition translated "on" in English often means "prior to" or "by" in Hebrew. The Bible is quite clear in many passages that God created everything in six days, not seven.

Genesis 2 does not mention the "Sabbath" nor does it refer to a religious feast day or any special institution. What it says is that God "rested on the seventh day." Because He is God, He never gets tired in the exercise of His power (Isaiah 40:28), nor does He ever sleep (Psalm 121:3-4). God "rested" to indicate that His work of creation was finished. He simply "ended His work."

The Seventh Day Was Designed by God to Be a Unique and Blessed Day

Genesis 2:3 says "God blessed the seventh day and sanctified it." The word "sanctified" means that God set this day apart from all other days. No day of the week was to be like the seventh day; it is special because of the blessing of God upon it.

Exodus 20:8-11 tells the children of Israel to remember this day. These words are a part of the Ten Commandments which God gave to the people of Israel through His servant Moses.

> Remember the Sabbath day, to keep it holy. Six days you shall labor and do all your work, but the seventh day is the Sabbath of the LORD your God. In it you shall do no work: you, nor your son, nor your daughter, nor your manservant, nor your maidservant, nor your cattle, nor your stranger who is within your gates. For in six days the LORD made the heavens and the earth, the sea, and all that is in them, and rested the seventh day. Therefore the LORD blessed the Sabbath day and hallowed it.

The seventh day is clearly called "the Sabbath of the LORD your God." The children of Israel were to remember this day and keep it holy; it was to be separated from all other days. The reason for this uniqueness? "For in six days the LORD made the heavens and the earth, the sea, and all that is in them, and rested the seventh day." That's the reason.

A fascinating insight into what was to be done on this special day is found in Psalm 92, a song written for the Sabbath day:

> It is good to give thanks to the LORD,
> And to sing praises to Your name, O Most High;
> To declare Your lovingkindness in the morning,
> And Your faithfulness every night,
> On an instrument of ten strings,
> On the lute,
> And on the harp,
> With harmonious sound.
> For You, LORD, have made me glad through Your
>   work;
> I will triumph in the works of Your hands.

Music, praise, giving of thanks—this is what God wants on His special Sabbath day, morning and night. Likewise in the Jewish laws of sacrifice, the Sabbath day received special attention (Numbers 28:9-10).

The Seventh Day Was Developed by God for Man's Benefit

God did not rest because He was tired. What He develops and teaches for the seventh day is done for man's benefit. When Moses recounts the Ten Commandments for Israel as they are about to enter the promised land (Deuteronomy 5), he adds the following: " 'Observe the Sabbath day . . . that your manservant and your maidservant may rest as well as you.' " No work is to be done by any person or any animal so that all "may rest."

Every person needs a regular rest from work. Unfortunately, some people seem to think they need several days of rest (even while on the job!). All work is to be done in six days, and then every person needs a break.

In Mark 2:27-28, Jesus Christ said: "The Sabbath was made for man, and not man for the Sabbath. Therefore the Son of Man is also Lord of the Sabbath." Jesus is not suggesting that every individual is free to use or abuse the Sabbath as he sees fit, but that Sabbath observance in the Old Testament was a beneficial privilege, not a mere legal point. It was not an end in itself, as the Pharisees seemed to think.

The purpose of the day of rest, the Sabbath day, was to relieve the people of Israel of their work for one day in seven in which they could worship God and refresh their physical bodies. That's good advice for any person living today!

The Seventh Day Was Dedicated to God

Exodus 31:15 tells us that the Sabbath day was "holy to the LORD," that is, set apart for the Lord's purposes and use: "Work shall be done for six days, but the seventh is the Sabbath of rest, holy to the LORD. Whoever does any work on the Sabbath day, he shall surely be put to death."

Earlier Moses had told the children of Israel as they began their wilderness journey out of the bondage of Egypt that God would feed them with manna from heaven (Exodus 16). However the Sabbath day was unique, a special day dedicated to the Lord. Because no manna would fall on the Sabbath, the children of Israel had to pick up twice as much on Friday as they would on other days.

The Seventh Day Was Demanded by God
as a Sign of His Covenant with the Children of Israel

The biblical evidence is that the Sabbath was established by God for the people of Israel and was to be celebrated as a weekly sign of the covenant God gave to Moses for His people Israel. Consider carefully the words of the Lord to Moses in Exodus 31:13-17:

> "Speak also to the children of Israel, saying: 'Surely My Sabbaths you shall keep, for it is a sign between Me and you throughout your generations, that you may know that I am the LORD who sanctifies you. You shall keep the Sabbath, therefore, for it is holy to you. Everyone who profanes it shall surely be put to death; for whoever does any work on it, that person shall be cut off from among his people. Work shall be done for six days, but the seventh is the Sabbath of rest, holy to the LORD. Whoever does any work on the Sabbath day, he shall surely be put to death. Therefore the children of Israel shall keep the Sabbath, to observe the Sabbath throughout their generations as a perpetual covenant. It is a sign between Me and the children of Israel forever; for in six days the LORD made the heavens and the earth, and on the seventh day He rested and was refreshed.'"

The Sabbath is not taught as a universal ordinance for all mankind. It was and is a specific institution for *the children of Israel.* As a sign of the covenant given to Moses, it was meant to last as long as that covenant would last.

Each of God's covenants has a sign. The covenant to Noah had the sign of the rainbow. The covenant to Abraham had the sign of circumcision. The Sabbath serves that function in relation to the covenant given to Moses.

The book of Hebrews in the New Testament argues that the covenant given to Moses has been supplanted by a new covenant based on the shed blood of Jesus Christ. We are "not under law but under grace" (Romans 6:14). Because we are now under a new covenant, there is no application of the old covenant's demands.

Christians who have taken the demands of the Sabbath day and applied it to Sunday have no biblical justification whatsoever for such teaching. The selection of Sunday as the worship day for Christians is not rooted in its connection to the Sabbath laws of the Old Testament. Christians celebrate their faith and worship the Lord on Sunday for reasons that are rooted in our Jewish heritage:

The feast of firstfruits always is celebrated on Sunday. Jesus Christ is called our "firstfruits" in 1 Corinthians 15:23, referring to His resurrection from the dead and the fact that this is our guarantee that we also shall rise from the dead. Every Sunday is a Christian celebration of the resurrection of Jesus Christ from the dead!

The feast of Pentecost always is celebrated on Sunday. The church of Jesus Christ was born on the feast of Pentecost, a fulfillment of that feast's activities. Two loaves of bread were waved by the priest on that day. These two loaves, representing Jew and Gentile, have now become one loaf. The two, Jew and Gentile, have now become "one new man" (Ephesians 2:11-18), thus guaranteeing access for both to the Father Himself. Acts 2:1 makes it quite clear when the church began. The Holy Spirit came in mighty power on that day, and it is by the Holy Spirit that we are all baptized into the one body of Jesus Christ, the church (1 Corinthians 12:13).

The Seventh Day Is Described as a Shadow of Things to Come

In Colossians 2:16-17 we learn of the relationship of the Sabbath to the future: "Therefore let no one judge you in food or in drink, or regarding a festival or a new moon or sabbaths, which are a shadow of things to come, but the substance is of Christ."

To attempt to transfer the signs and institutions of the old covenant to the new covenant—equating circumcision with baptism, Passover with communion, priest with pastor, temple with church, tithing with giving, Sabbath with Sunday—is not scriptural, and is in fact a violation of clear teaching in the New Testament. Sabbaths are a part of what is described as "a shadow of things to come." It is not the reality. The substance is found in the Messiah. He is the fulfillment of Old Testament types, rituals, and celebrations for the believer today.

The Seventh Day Was Designated to Represent
Salvation by Faith apart from Works

One of the most fascinating discussions concerning the Sabbath day is found in Hebrews 4:1-11. The point of this passage is to teach that salvation is by faith and not by the works of the law. The contrasts and comparisons of this passage help us to see the original purpose of the seventh day of creation.

> Therefore, since a promise remains of entering His rest, let us fear lest any of you seem to have come short of it. For indeed the gospel was preached to us as well as to them; but the word which they heard did not profit them, not being mixed with faith in those who heard it. For we who have believed do enter that rest, as He has said:
>
> > "So I swore in My wrath,
> > 'They shall not enter My rest,' "
>
> although the works were finished from the foundation of the world. For He has spoken in a certain place of the seventh day in this way: "And God rested on the seventh day from all His works"; and again in this place: "They shall not enter My rest." Since therefore it remains that some must enter it, and those to whom it was first preached did not enter because of disobedience, again He designates a certain day, saying in David, "Today," after such a long time, as it has been said:
>
> > "Today, if you will hear His voice,
> > Do not harden your hearts."
>
> For if Joshua had given them rest, then He would not afterward have spoken of another day. There remains therefore a rest for the people of God. For he who has entered His rest has himself also ceased from his works as God did from His.
>
> Let us therefore be diligent to enter that rest, lest anyone fall after the same example of disobedience.

The teaching of this passage is remarkable as it relates to the meaning of the seventh day. The book of Genesis speaks of God's rest on the seventh day, and Psalm 95, written by King

David four hundred years after Israel's wilderness wanderings, speaks of the children of Israel not being able to enter the rest of God, the land of Canaan, the promised land. David makes an appeal to the people of God to hear the voice of God and to be careful not to harden their hearts like the children of Israel did in the wilderness. Obviously, if the children of Israel had entered the rest of God at the time when Joshua conquered the land of Canaan, then David's words would be meaningless. As Hebrews 4:8-9 argues, there still remains a rest for the people of God, something more than what happened when Joshua conquered Canaan.

The whole point of this passage is that the seventh day, on which God rested from His work of creation, represents the salvation of the believer. We enter into the rest of God, a peace that passes all understanding, a right relationship to God, the moment we believe the gospel (Hebrews 4:2). If we think we are saved by our works, we will fall "after the same example of disobedience" (v. 11) demonstrated by the children of Israel during the wilderness wanderings. They trusted themselves, their own works, instead of believing God concerning the possession of the promised land.

This story is powerful—a vivid analogy! Exactly where do we stand in relationship to what has just been said? Are we like the children of Israel in the wilderness, now wandering around spiritually, emotionally, intellectually, because we have not believed God and His Word? Are we trying to earn our way into God's rest? Do we believe that peace with God is found by human effort and performance? The Bible teaches otherwise.

Chapter 6

The Garden of Eden

(2:4-17)

After examining a travel brochure for one of the world's most beautiful and exotic tropical islands in the South Pacific, my wife said, "It's a paradise!" That, of course, meant that we ought to make plans to visit as soon as possible.

There are some beautiful places in this world, in spite of our pollution of the environment. But often a so-called natural disaster, such as an earthquake, tornado, or hurricane, will turn a potential paradise into a disaster area.

Before earthquakes, tornadoes, hurricanes, and human desecration could ever begin, there was a beautiful place on planet earth, unlike anything our eyes have seen. It was indeed a paradise. It was called "a garden" and was located in a place called "Eden." Genesis 2:4-17 describes this beautiful place, the original home of humanity on planet earth. This is where it all began.

> **⁴This is the history of the heavens and the earth when they were created, in the day that the LORD God made the earth and the heavens, ⁵before any plant of the field was in the earth and before any herb of the field had grown. For the LORD God had not caused it to rain on the earth, and there was no man to till the ground; ⁶but a mist went up from the earth and watered the whole face of the ground. ⁷And the LORD God formed man of the dust of the ground, and breathed into his nostrils the breath of life; and man became a living being.**

> **⁸The LORD God planted a garden eastward in Eden, and there He put the man whom He had formed.**

⁹**And out of the ground the LORD God made every tree grow that is pleasant to the sight and good for food. The tree of life was also in the midst of the garden, and the tree of the knowledge of good and evil.**

¹⁰**Now a river went out of Eden to water the garden, and from there it parted and became four riverheads. ¹¹The name of the first is Pishon; it is the one which encompasses the whole land of Havilah, where there is gold. ¹²And the gold of that land is good. Bdellium and the onyx stone are there. ¹³The name of the second river is Gihon; it is the one which encompasses the whole land of Cush. ¹⁴The name of the third river is Hiddekel; it is the one which goes toward the east of Assyria. The fourth river is the Euphrates.**

¹⁵**Then the LORD God took the man and put him in the garden of Eden to tend and keep it. ¹⁶And the LORD God commanded the man, saying, "Of every tree of the garden you may freely eat; ¹⁷but of the tree of the knowledge of good and evil you shall not eat, for in the day that you eat of it you shall surely die."**

The Planting of a Garden

The word *Eden* means "delight" in Hebrew. The place where God placed humanity was an absolute delight. We are told that it was "eastward." Without any further descriptions, that statement would normally refer to land that would be east of Israel, the centerpiece of God's prophetic plan. The rivers that are mentioned suggest that the place of humanity's beginnings was the Mesopotamian valley, the area known as "the fertile crescent."

Isaiah 51:3 remarks about God's restoration of Israel in the future and relates it to the beauty of Eden in the past:

For the LORD will comfort Zion,
He will comfort all her waste places;
He will make her wilderness like Eden,
And her desert like the garden of the LORD;
Joy and gladness will be found in it,
Thanksgiving and the voice of melody.

The phrase "the garden of the LORD" is a description of Eden. It is possible that the words "joy and gladness" and "thanksgiving and the voice of melody," in addition to describing the mood in restored Zion, depict the atmosphere in the original garden of Eden.

According to Genesis 2:8, the garden was designed for the man God formed. God's intention was that the human beings He created would live in a beautiful, healthful environment. Verse 9 says that the trees in the garden were "pleasant to the sight" and "good for food." Beautiful surroundings and physical sustenance for man's health were available every day in the garden of Eden.

First Timothy 4:3-5 speaks of "foods which God created to be received with thanksgiving by those who believe and know the truth." We should be thankful for the food God has provided for our nourishment and health. Do you pray before you eat your meals? Rarely does one see that simple act of thanksgiving being done. The Bible warns that we should not forget to thank the Lord for His good gifts to us, including our food (Deuteronomy 8). The Lord gives, and the Lord can take it all away (Job 1:21). We should give thanks for the simple things of life, especially for the food that nourishes and sustains us.

The Purpose of Two Special Trees

Two unusual trees were placed by God in the original garden of Eden, the tree of life and the tree of the knowledge of good and evil.

The tree of life. The "tree of life" was located in the central place of the garden of Eden (2:9). Some believe the tree is simply an illustration or a symbol of life itself. It is certainly an unusual tree in that it is characterized by life or produces life. All trees designed to produce food for humanity are in a sense trees of life. They give us food that sustains us. But this tree is different.

When Adam and Eve are finally expelled from the garden of Eden because of their sin, it is fascinating to read that the Lord God "placed cherubim [angels] at the east of the garden of Eden, and a flaming sword which turned every way, to guard the way to the tree of life" (Genesis 3:24). This tree of life is so special that humanity was forbidden to have access to it after sinning against God.

In the book of Revelation, the last book of the Bible, we find letters to seven churches that existed during the latter days of the first century A.D. To the church in Ephesus a promise was given to all those who were true believers—"I will give to eat from the tree of life, which is in the midst of the Paradise of God (Revelation 2:7)."

The "paradise of God" is no longer in the garden of Eden but, according to 2 Corinthians 12:2-4, is located in the "third heaven," the place where God dwells and where the heavenly city is presently found. The tree of life is once again planted "in the midst of the Paradise of God." It is the central feature.

In Revelation 22:2 the tree of life is mentioned again and is found in the heavenly city that God is preparing for true believers. It yields fruit once a month and its leaves are for "the healing of the nations." Quite an unusual tree!

Putting all of this together, it seems that the tree of life represents, whether by symbol or by literal tree, the gift of life, both physical and spiritual, a life that will never end—eternal life, which Romans 6:23 calls "the gift of God." God was merciful to Adam and Eve in keeping them away from this tree after they had sinned. Partaking of it would have caused them to be eternally separated from God, permanently sealed in their fate without hope of recovery or redemption.

The words of Revelation make it clear that only true believers will ever enjoy the benefits of this amazing tree, a tree which grants eternal life to all who put their faith and trust in the living God and His Messiah, Jesus Christ our Lord.

The tree of the knowledge of good and evil. The second tree that receives attention in the garden of Eden symbolizes humanity's moral understanding. "Good and evil" are moral concepts that are dependent upon the will and revelation of God, not the experiences or feelings of humanity. This tree was "off limits" to Adam and Eve. They could enjoy every tree of the garden but this one. It was a spiritual test involving two things:

1. A specific command—"Of every tree of the garden you may freely eat; but of the tree of the knowledge of good and evil you shall not eat" (2:16-17). There was a positive aspect to this original command of God—"of every tree . . . you may freely eat." But the negative part which prohibited them taking the fruit of this one tree became the point of their greatest temptation.

Such is the way of humanity to this present day. There is so much to enjoy in life, but we seem to gravitate by natural tendency and desire to that which God forbids. Though we should understand that His commands are for our good, we question His authority and rules and seek by whatever means possible to violate them. It is a part of the rebellion that lies in every heart.

2. *A serious consequence*—"for in the day that you eat of it you shall surely die" (2:17). According to Genesis 5:3, Adam was 130 years old when his son, Seth, was born. Adam died when he was 930 years old (5:5). It appears that Adam lived for over eight hundred years after his sin of eating the forbidden fruit. Did the consequence of death come to Adam the day he ate of the forbidden fruit? Certainly not if it meant that he would die physically that same day. The death that Adam and Eve experienced the day they took of the forbidden fruit was spiritual, not physical. Physical death (which did occur later) is the consequence of spiritual death.

The Bible says that some people who are physically alive are spiritually dead because of sin (Ephesians 2:1-3). Our sins separate us from God so that He will not hear or respond to us (Isaiah 59:1-2). Unless the problem of spiritual death, our separation from God, is solved during our physical lifetime, we face the terrible reality of eternal separation from God. When physical death occurs, there is no hope of sharing eternal life with the God Who made you.

The Problem of Water

One of the interesting facts about this beautiful paradise of God is the way God provided its water supply. According to Genesis 2:5 no rain had fallen on the earth as yet. Instead, "a mist went up from the earth and watered the whole face of the ground" (v. 6). The water came from the ground itself.

The garden is watered by a river (v. 10) which splits into four "riverheads" after it comes out of the garden of Eden. The names of the four rivers are given with some information as to their geographical locations.

Pishon—"the one which encompasses the whole land of Havilah, where there is gold. And the gold of that land is good. Bdellium and the onyx stone are there" (vv. 11-12). Jewish commentators who have tried to identify this river have proposed the Nile River in Egypt as well as the Ganges River in India. Havilah was one of the sons of Cush, a grandson of Noah (Genesis 10:7).

Gihon—"the one which encompasses the whole land of Cush" (v. 13). Cush was the father of Nimrod (Genesis 10:8-12) whose empire covered much of ancient Mesopotamia.

Hiddekel—"the one which goes toward the east of Assyria" (v. 14). The Hebrew word refers to the Tigris River upon which the ancient city of Nineveh was built. In the Hebrew text of Daniel 10:4, which speaks of the Tigris River, the word is *Hiddekel.*

Euphrates—"the fourth river" (v. 14). There is no identifying description in the text concerning this river. The Euphrates is mentioned many times in the Bible and is one of the greatest rivers on the face of the earth. The Tigris and the Euphrates both flow into the Persian Gulf, and the Euphrates River was a natural boundary between the east and the west in ancient times. It is the river upon which the ancient city of Babylon was built.

The water supply of the garden was sufficient to cause "every tree" to grow that was "pleasant to the sight and good for food" (v. 9). God had provided all that Adam and Eve would ever need. A perfect environment, a true Paradise, a place where humans and animals could live together, sustained by the plants and vegetation God had created for their enjoyment and health.

Since then we have done much to ruin this planet. Ecological disregard has reaped a terrible harvest, with pollution of water and food supplies around the world becoming an increasing concern to scientists and health experts. Modern technology and industrial pursuits have added to the frightening possibility that no product or environment may be safe for humanity. The Bible speaks of environmental problems increasing in the last days of planet earth. Pollution will become widespread, and death will occur to animals, plants, and humans.

Is There Any Hope for Planet Earth?

The Bible teaches that God will one day create new heavens and a new earth. The Hebrew prophet Isaiah spoke these words of hope over twenty-five hundred years ago:

> For behold, I create new heavens and a new earth;
> And the former shall not be remembered or come to mind.
> But be glad and rejoice forever in what I create.
> (Isaiah 65:17-18)

The prophet Ezekiel (five hundred years before Jesus Christ) spoke of the day when the waters of the Dead Sea "will be healed" and the fish in it "will be of the same kinds as the fish of the Great Sea, exceedingly many" (Ezekiel 47:9-10).

The New Testament book of Revelation speaks eloquently of a new world that is coming. In Revelation 21:1, the writer was given a vision of "a new heaven and a new earth, for the first heaven and the first earth had passed away." And God Himself says: "Behold, I make all things new" (21:5).

One day an ecological miracle will take place—the environment will experience a mighty transformation, and God will set up His kingdom on earth with His Son, Jesus Christ our Lord, ruling as King of kings and Lord of lords! The Bible teaches that every knee will bow to Him and every tongue will confess that He is Lord (Philippians 2:9-11). In order to be saved and share in the glory and joy of that future day, each person must make a commitment or decision. In Romans 10:9-10 we read these powerful words:

> If you confess with your mouth the Lord Jesus and believe in your heart that God has raised Him from the dead, you will be saved. For with the heart one believes to righteousness, and with the mouth confession is made to salvation.

Have you made that personal commitment to Jesus Christ? Your eternal destiny is determined by your response to Him.

Chapter 7
Sex, Marriage, and Human Relationships
(2:18-25)

Our study of origins gives us many significant insights. Few are more important than the insight we can gain into our sexuality and our appreciation and respect for male-female relationships. The world of humanity is composed of males and females; that is the divine order and plan. God is delighted with His plan and expects us to understand it and relate to it by His principles and instructions.

The woman was not an afterthought of God. In Genesis 1:27 we read "male and female He created them." God's work of creating the human race included from the beginning the unique and wonderful distinctions of male and female. There was never any intention on the part of God to make all humans the same sex. God was delighted with each one and desired both to grace His universe and bring joy to His heart.

The beautiful story of the creation of the woman is the basis for all accurate understanding of male and female relationships, including the beauty and joy of sex. Genesis 2:18-25 gives us the following details:

> [18]And the LORD God said, "It is not good that man should be alone; I will make him a helper comparable to him." [19]Out of the ground the LORD God formed every beast of the field and every bird of the air, and brought them to Adam to see what he would call them. And whatever Adam called each living creature, that was its name. [20]So Adam gave names to all cattle, to the birds of the air, and to every beast of the field.

But for Adam there was not found a helper comparable to him. [21]**And the LORD God caused a deep sleep to fall on Adam, and he slept; and He took one of his ribs, and closed up the flesh in its place.** [22]**Then the rib which the LORD God had taken from man he made into a woman, and He brought her to the man.** [23]**And Adam said:**

> **"This is now bone of my bones**
> **And flesh of my flesh;**
> **She shall be called Woman,**
> **Because she was taken out of Man."**

[24]**Therefore a man shall leave his father and mother and be joined to his wife, and they shall become one flesh.** [25]**And they were both naked, the man and his wife, and were not ashamed.**

God's Purpose in Creating the Woman

Man's need is determined by God from the beginning. He knows best what we need because He is the One Who made us. The woman was designed by God to meet needs that existed in the man. Though the man was a part of the "very good" creation of God, it is obvious from the beginning that without the woman, the man is incomplete from God's point of view. Our world in its desire to prove its self-reliance and independence is working against the original purposes of God Himself. No wonder we make such a mess of human relationships and responsibilities.

God created the woman to explain the basic need of every person. Genesis 2:18 says, "It is not good that man should be alone." One cannot help but notice the striking contrast between the original creation of God that is called "very good" (Genesis 1:31), and this statement announcing that something is "not good." From the beginning God intended to teach all people that it is not good to be isolated from other human beings. You may want to be alone at times, but to live that way, without human contact and personal relationships, is not the original intention of God.

Proverbs 18:1 states,

> A man who isolates himself seeks his own desire;
> He rages against all wise judgment.

The truth is, we all need friends, people with whom we can share our ideas, dreams, goals, burdens, struggles, and needs.

Men can be close friends with other men, and women with women. We are all aware of that fact. The interesting thing to understand from the point of God's original creation is that He started with male and female, not two members of the same sex. There is a need in all males for female companionship and relationship, and the same need in females for male friendship. Without God's laws governing these relationships, society would be without order, destructive and harmful to the very relationships which we all desire and need. When self-gratification becomes the motive for male-female relationships and the only motive is sexual, the relationship can easily deteriorate and damage our self-esteem and respect. Closeness and intimacy with another person can be quickly lost when selfish desire or sensual gratification is the only basis for the relationship.

The need is companionship, an intimacy that does not necessarily demand sexual involvement, although, as we shall see, that is a vital part of human need for which God has made adequate provision.

God created the woman to establish the motivation behind all male-female relationships. God said "I will make him a helper comparable to him." The original plan of God is beautifully portrayed by that simple word "helper." Male-female relationships would greatly improve for all of us if it was our sincere desire to be a "helper" rather than a hindrance. To give rather than receive more accurately fulfills God's original purpose for male-female relationships. The goal is not to use people to meet our needs, but to do all we can to help the other person become all that God wants that person to be.

This helper role is clarified somewhat by the phrase "comparable to him." The New American Standard Bible says "suitable" to him. There is a certain interdependency that is present when male-female relationships are what God intended them to be. When the male tries to dominate or suppress the female, making her a slave to his every wish and demand, God's purpose is violated and great harm comes to the emotional responses of the female as well as to the relationship that might have been between them.

God's Process for Creating the Woman

Everything God did and continues to do is rooted in His purpose and plan. Nothing is done by accident or coincidence. Consider the following three things about the unique process God chose to bring the woman into existence.

God's original plan was deeply impressed upon Adam by the task of naming the animals. In order to help Adam see his need of a helper, God brought all the animals to him so that Adam could give them names. Adam did not have to round them up; that would have been a difficult, if not impossible, task. God simply caused them to come to Adam. Adam "gave names to all cattle, to the birds of the air, and to every beast of the field" (2:20). Fish were excluded. Adam's ability to do what he did is indeed remarkable given the number and variety of animals he had to name.

In this process, Adam became aware that in the animal world, God had given companions. The light dawns on his brilliant and innocent mind that he was alone—every creature had a friend or helper except himself! What a fascinating way for God to open up Adam's heart and mind to his need for companionship. Maybe those of us who try to walk alone should be forced to go through a similar process in order to get the point.

God's creative power was demonstrated in a unique way so that humanity would understand the special relationship He intended between male and female. God's activity in creating the woman is clearly presented: (1) He caused a deep sleep, (2) He took one of Adam's ribs, (3) He closed up the flesh, (4) He made a woman out of the rib, and (5) He brought the woman to the man. No thought of evolution here or millions of years to complete the task. All it takes is the hand of God Himself!

When God took the rib out of man's side (that's what I call "prime rib"!), He intended to teach the entire human race about the relationship of a man to a woman. If He intended for the man to dominate the woman as a master would his slave, He could have taken a bone out of Adam's foot. If He wanted the woman to be superior to the man, He could have removed the main bone structure of Adam's head. He did neither. He took one of his ribs, a bone from the man's side, so that no one could misunderstand the special relationship God wanted for the man and woman—partners, side by side, dependent upon each other, helpers and friends.

In Genesis 2:22, the Hebrew word for "made" implies a construction project. The New American Standard Bible translates it "fashioned." God crafted a woman out of a man's rib.

God's divine purpose was revealed in Adam's response to what God had created. One can imagine the joy and excitement in Adam's heart when he first glanced at what God had made for him. Here was a perfect woman fashioned by God Himself.

Adam was immediately aware of the physical compatibility he had with this creature God designed: "This is now bone of my bones / And flesh of my flesh." A female is the physical counterpart of the male—an obvious fact, even if you've not had a course in anatomy!

First Corinthians 11:8-12 expands on this unique physical relationship between man and woman:

> For man is not from woman, but woman from man. Nor was man created for the woman, but woman for the man. For this reason the woman ought to have a symbol of authority on her head, because of the angels. Nevertheless, neither is man independent of woman, nor woman independent of man, in the Lord. For as the woman was from the man, even so the man also is through the woman; but all things are from God.

God was behind the whole process—"all things are from God." He made the woman from the man, but then ordained that every man would be born of a woman. It is important for every man and woman to understand this interdependency. The fact that a man comes out of a woman's womb establishes the dependency of a male upon a female. The fact that the woman was originally designed from the man's rib is intended by God to show the female's dependency upon the male. God never intended us to live in isolation from one another.

In the marriage relationship, this truth of "bone of my bones and flesh of my flesh" is not only an obvious physical relationship, but also becomes the basis for teaching the personal responsibility of the husband to care for his wife:

> So husbands ought to love their own wives as their own bodies; he who loves his wife loves himself. For no one ever hated his own flesh, but nourishes and cherishes it, just as the Lord does the church. For we

> are members of His body, of His flesh and of His bones. "For this reason a man shall leave his father and mother and be joined to his wife, and the two shall become one flesh."
>
> (Ephesians 5:28-31)

The husband is responsible to nourish and cherish his wife as though she were his own flesh because she is bone of his bones and flesh of his flesh. The woman in a marriage is considered one with the man, and vice versa.

The Principles God Established in Making Male and Female One Flesh

The present cultural attitude toward marriage and family is not fulfilling God's original plan and purpose. We have gotten away from the principles and values of the Bible and have substituted our own opinions and allowed our selfish desires to dictate moral values. Divorce is the "creative alternative" if things don't work out the way we wanted. Marriage is fine if it proves financially beneficial or personally satisfactory.

God never intended for all men to get married, nor did he intend for all women to walk the aisle. Jesus Christ said, "there are eunuchs who were born thus from their mother's womb, and there are eunuchs who were made eunuchs by men, and there are eunuchs who have made themselves eunuchs for the kingdom of heaven's sake" (Matthew 19:12). The apostle Paul honors and exalts the single state in 1 Corinthians 7 and urges those who are able to do so to stay single. Marriage is not a requirement for every man and woman.

Although marriage is not for everyone, male and female relationships are. Each of us needs friendships with members of the opposite sex. Our society makes that difficult. By our media promotions and marketing we suggest that the goal is sexual relationship, not social or emotional companionship and friendship. The Bible teaches otherwise.

Yet if Adam and Eve had been designed to be single, then the human race would have been limited to two people! One of the greatest and most rewarding male-female relationships is the one that culminates in marriage, a relationship that regards the man and the woman as "one flesh."

Three basic principles for marriage were established by God from the beginning.

Marital fidelity—"A man shall leave his father and mother and be joined to his wife." In contrast to other male-female relationships which can involve several people as friends and helpers, a decision to be married requires loyalty and commitment to one person. This does not mean we cannot or should not relate as friends with other people, but it does restrict and limit the nature of our involvement with others and sets up a unique priority system for those who marry. One's spouse comes first.

Consider the words of Jesus Christ on this matter of leaving your parents and cleaving to your wife:

> Have you not read that He who made them at the beginning "made them male and female," and said, "For this reason a man shall leave his father and mother and be joined to his wife, and the two shall become one flesh"? So then, they are no longer two but one flesh. Therefore what God has joined together, let not man separate.
>
> (Matthew 19:4-6)

God established the commitment we call marriage. He "has joined together" the male and female in physical oneness. He intends that no one break up this relationship. It is to last throughout a person's lifetime on earth. Romans 7:1-3 comments on the extent of the marital commitment:

> Or do you not know, brethren (for I speak to those who know the law), that the law has dominion over a man as long as he lives? For the woman who has a husband is bound by the law to her husband as long as he lives. But if the husband dies, she is released from the law of her husband. So then if, while her husband lives, she marries another man, she will be called an adulteress; but if her husband dies, she is free from that law, so that she is no adulteress, though she has married another man.
>
> (cf. 1 Corinthians 7:39)

Strong words! The marital vow should clearly state "until death do us part!"

If we are reading this passage carefully, the purpose of marriage is first and foremost a commitment to faithful companionship, fulfilling God's original intention for man and woman. The command to have children, another purpose of marriage, was given to both Adam and Eve according to Genesis 1:27-28. Eve was obviously around to hear that one. But before she came into existence, God established the purpose of companionship by what He said to Adam.

Sexual unity—"and they shall become one flesh." The purposes of marriage begin with faithful companionship and sexual relationship. After these are understood God adds the purpose of conception of children.

The meaning of the phrase "one flesh" is sexual unity, although many marriage books and seminars have expanded the idea to include emotional and spiritual oneness. Of course, emotional and spiritual oneness are important, but they are not all that is meant by the phrase "one flesh." Sexual involvement is a vital part of the meaning of this phrase.

The primary restriction upon male-female relationships is that of sexual involvement. In God's wisdom and plan, He has commanded that sexual unity occur only within the bonds of marriage. Since the sexual relationship demands a great deal of trust and loyalty to be fulfilling and satisfying to our emotional makeup, it necessitates a promise of fidelity between husband and wife. The marriage vows should always include, "to forsake all others and to cleave to him/her alone."

Hebrews 13:4 reveals God's approval of sexual unity within marriage and His prohibition of sexual activity outside of marriage: "Marriage is honorable among all, and the bed undefiled; but fornicators and adulterers God will judge." Proverbs 5:18-20 makes sexual unity and satisfaction an experience only married people should know:

> Let your fountain be blessed,
> And rejoice with the wife of your youth.
> As a loving deer and a graceful doe,
> Let her breasts satisfy you at all times;
> And always be enraptured with her love.
> For why should you, my son, be enraptured by an
> immoral woman,
> And be embraced in the arms of a seductress?

God intends that those among us who are given strong sexual desire should be happy, satisfied, and sexually fulfilled. He says that the only way this can occur is within the bonds and commitment of marriage. Only within marriage can true sexual pleasure and satisfaction occur. Quite a contrast to today's society with its sexual freedoms and promiscuity! First Corinthians 6:16-18 reveals the seriousness of having sexual relations outside of marriage:

> Or do you not know that he who is joined to a harlot is one body with her? For "The two," He says, "shall become one flesh." But he who is joined to the Lord is one spirit with Him. Flee sexual immorality. Every sin that a man does is outside the body, but he who commits sexual immorality sins against his own body.

Sin affects our emotional and spiritual relationship to God. But one sin will affect our physical nature as well—sexual immorality. While commentators disagree as to what these consequences might be, the Bible implies loss of sexual vitality and enjoyment as one immediate result (Proverbs 5:15-20). Another possibility is sexual disease, a result Romans 1:27 may well be referring to.

It is well known that having sexual intercourse outside of marriage diminishes the enduring love and commitment of two people to each other. What at first seems to bind them together (sexual intercourse) will later drive them apart because of the lack of commitment, trust, and responsibility which only the accountability of marriage can provide.

Complete intimacy—"And they were both naked, the man and his wife, and were not ashamed." Intimacy is one of the most fulfilling and rewarding aspects of a committed relationship between a man and a woman. In marriage, the level of intimacy can be deeper and more intimate than any other male-female relationship. Often this is not the case because the couple has failed to understand this important principle in marriage or simply does not take the time to work on it in their relationship with each other.

The word *naked* implies more than nudity. It speaks of transparency, of having nothing to hide. Hebrews 4:13 says, "And there is no creature hidden from His sight, but all things are naked and open to the eyes of Him to whom we must give account." Openness, transparency, honesty—these are essentials of intimacy in any human relationship. They become most important and serious within the marital bond. Couples will hurt their marriage and weaken their relationship with each other if they do not develop and enjoy an open and transparent relationship.

In addition to transparency, complete intimacy within marriage also involves purity. When a marriage is characterized by purity, there is no reason to be ashamed or embarrassed. In our spiritual relationship with the Lord, this concept becomes quite apparent. In 1 John 2:28-3:3 there is admonition to believers to "not be ashamed" at the coming of Christ. After speaking of this great hope and anticipation of every believer, the writer says, "And everyone who has this hope in Him purifies himself" (3:3).

The issues of sex, marriage, and human relationships are rooted in the plan and purpose of God Himself. Many of us lack fulfillment and meaning in these areas because we have not consulted the God Who made us and the only One Who really knows what we are like and what we need. We stumble through life making a mess of these matters and then wonder what went wrong. We need to get back to the God of the Bible and commit our lives and future to Him. He is the God of origins, and His design and purpose is the only plan to follow for true happiness and peace of mind!

Chapter 8
The Fall of the Human Race
(3:1-24)

The garden of Eden was a perfect environment and filled with every imaginable resource for man's happiness. It was a gift from the Creator and was intended to demonstrate to His creatures the nature and extent of His love and care. But something went wrong! The beauty of the garden turned into a nightmare. The simplicity and freshness of humanity's relationship to God became selfish, ugly, and deceitful.

The story of Genesis 3 is an essential part of our understanding of origins—where we came from, why we are now the way we are.

The Temptation
(3:1-6)

The Bible teaches that Adam and Eve were tempted to disobey God. The result of the temptation was a severe loss of all that the garden of Eden provided and promised.

> ¹Now the serpent was more cunning than any beast of the field which the LORD God had made. And he said to the woman, "Has God indeed said, 'You shall not eat of every tree of the garden'?" ²And the woman said to the serpent, "We may eat the fruit of the trees of the garden; ³but of the fruit of the tree which is in the midst of the garden, God has said, 'You shall not eat it, nor shall you touch it, lest you die.'" ⁴And the serpent said to the woman, "You will not surely die. ⁵For God knows that in the day you eat of it your eyes

will be opened, and you will be like God, knowing good and evil." ⁶So when the woman saw that the tree was good for food, that it was pleasant to the eyes, and a tree desirable to make one wise, she took of its fruit and ate. She also gave to her husband with her, and he ate.

The Cause behind the Temptation

Why do people do what they do? That is a fundamental question. The temptation of Adam and Eve resulted in their fall, a plunge into moral and spiritual depravity, a new attitude of selfishness and rebellion against the God Who made them. What caused all of this to happen when everything seemed so special and wonderful in the garden of Eden?

God was not the cause of the temptation. The Bible makes this point quite clear so that no person can accuse God of being cruel or unjust in His plan or His actions. We read about this fact in James 1:13-15:

> Let no one say when he is tempted, "I am tempted by God"; for God cannot be tempted by evil, nor does He Himself tempt anyone. But each one is tempted when he is drawn away by his own desires and enticed. Then, when desire has conceived, it gives birth to sin; and sin, when it is full-grown, brings forth death.

The Bible tells us in Hebrews 6:18 that it is impossible for God to lie. God does not sin nor does He tempt any human being to sin!

Man was not the cause of the temptation. Adam and Eve had no knowledge of good and evil (according to the opening verses of Genesis 3) until they ate of the fruit of the tree. Romans 5:12 tells us that sin "entered" the world through the disobedience of Adam. That implies that the cause was someone or something other than Adam himself. We are not trying to get Adam "off the hook." He sinned, and that is clear. However, he is not the cause of his own temptation and neither is Eve the cause (though some men like to believe that the woman is responsible for the temptation!). Eve was tempted, but she is not the cause of her own temptation.

The devil was the original cause of the temptation. Genesis 3 does not mention the devil or call him by his name Satan. It refers to "the serpent" three times in the first six verses. Second Corinthians 11:3 states that "the serpent deceived Eve by his craftiness." Revelation 12:9 speaks of "the great dragon" that was cast out of heaven, and calls him "that serpent of old . . . the Devil and Satan, who deceives the whole world."

The deceiver of the whole world is the devil or Satan. The fact that he appeared as a beautiful animal and talked with Eve is no surprise. He is able to transform himself into various forms, including human appearances, in order to accomplish his wicked schemes (2 Corinthians 11:13-15). Ephesians 6 speaks of the "wiles of the devil" (v. 11) and of the "fiery darts of the wicked one" (v. 16).

Jesus calls Satan a "murderer" and a "liar" (John 8:44). The apostle John says "He who sins is of the devil, for the devil has sinned from the beginning" (1 John 3:8). Paul calls him the "god of this age" who blinds us to the truth of the gospel (2 Corinthians 4:4) and the "prince of the power of the air, the spirit who now works in the sons of disobedience" (Ephesians 2:2). The Bible tells us that the result of his work is that we seek to fulfill the desires of the flesh and the mind.

While we all are responsible for the choices we make in life, and are thus accountable to God, the temptations are the work of the enemy, the devil. He will bait us and entice us with a multitude of attractive and alluring sights and activities. He deceives us into thinking that these things are not harmful or destructive. But, never forget, he is also called "Abaddon"—the destroyer (Revelation 9:11), and his motive is to ruin your life, not to bless you.

The Character of the Temptation

Understanding that the devil is the cause behind temptation is one thing, but comprehending what temptation is like is quite another. Most of us have our own ideas as to what is tempting or not. But just because something is tempting to us does not mean it is tempting to someone else. Also, what may not seem tempting to us may in fact be the very thing that brings our downfall. The devil is crafty and fully aware of our weaknesses and inconsistencies.

According to 1 Corinthians 10:13, no temptation is greater than we can bear. We often say with a degree of amusement, "I can resist anything but temptation!" The truth is, we have the ability to say "yes" or "no" to temptation. James 1:14 teaches that "each one is tempted when he is drawn away by his own desires."

The original temptation of Adam and Eve suggests a pattern characteristic of most temptations:

Temptation appears in a form that deceives. The devil and his demons are able to transform themselves into that which is attractive and good (2 Corinthians 11:14-15). It is an incredible thought that people who appear to be righteous and good in their lifestyles may be inhabited or empowered to appear that way by demons! If that tactic is necessary to deceive a person, then that is what the devil will use. Many false teachings that are in direct conflict with biblical truth have been accepted readily by people because of the appearance of good and righteous living on the part of adherents to that teaching.

Many people believe they will easily recognize temptation when they see it. That is utter nonsense! The Bible speaks of deception as the basic factor in temptation. Eve was deceived by Satan when he used an animal to speak to her. She had no reason to doubt that such a thing could occur. She lived in a beautiful environment where animals and humans enjoyed a relationship that was not built on fear or hostility. Since she and Adam could talk, why should it be so surprising if one of the animals would talk? The serpent was cursed to crawl in the dust which means that it was not "snake-like" in the beginning. Eve was clearly deceived (1 Timothy 2:14).

Temptation casts doubt on the Word of God. What the serpent did is a vital part of our understanding of temptation. He cast doubt on what God had said ("Has God indeed said . . . ?") in order to break down Eve's resistance to disobedience. Satan implies that Eve must have heard it wrong—surely God would not have said such a thing! How interesting that the devil phrases it the way he does. He did not say, "Why would God keep you from eating the fruit of one tree?" It was couched in more deceptive words as he implied that God would not let her eat of all the trees of the garden. But, let's face it, the issue was one tree, not "every tree of the garden." The devil's words were misleading, and that is the way temptation always comes.

Something is right or wrong because God has declared it to be so. Morality in our culture is so difficult because we allow humanity to make the decision as to what is moral or immoral. That decision rests with God, not us. What is moral to one man may be quite immoral to another.

The devil's tactic is always the same—he must get us to doubt and question the veracity and authority of God's Word. Once that happens, it is quite simple to lead people into sinning against God and one another.

Temptation causes us to reinterpret what God has said. Once the devil casts doubt on what God said, the next part of temptation is to cause us to reinterpret what God has said. At this point, most of us are ready for a fall! The moment we decide what God *really* meant, we are in the midst of temptation and unless checked soon, we will fall.

Eve's temptation involves at least two things at this critical point:

1. She leaves out one of God's words. She said, "We may eat the fruit of the trees of the garden." However, in the original directive from the Lord in Genesis 2:16, God said "Of every tree of the garden you may *freely* eat." Perhaps some would argue that this is a minor point and not worth mentioning.

Yet the word Eve left out expresses the love and character of our Lord. He is a God of grace, giving to us "freely" all things to enjoy (Romans 8:32). We are often tempted to experience the very things God has prohibited, rather than to enjoy the wonderful things He has given to us. All of His restrictions upon us are for our blessing, not to prevent us from having fun or a good time. When we think otherwise, we are playing into the devil's hand.

2. She adds to God's words. Eve said, "God has said, 'You shall not eat it, *nor shall you touch it.*' " But God never said that she could not touch it. Eve added to what God had said. Genesis 2:17 tells us what God said and it was simply "you shall not eat." There was not one word about touching the fruit.

Proverbs 30:5-6 warns about adding to God's words:

> Every word of God is pure;
> He is a shield to those who put their trust in Him.
> Do not add to His words,
> Lest He reprove you, and you be found a liar.

Eve had already bought the devil's temptation. His questioning of God's love and provision by referring to His restriction has now caused Eve to present Him in a worse light. God is so punitive in his ways, Eve thought, that He will not even let us touch the fruit—what harm could come from touching it, much less eating it? It is quite simple to see how temptation works, though at the time most of us are not aware that it is happening to us.

Temptation denies that we will suffer any consequences for disobedience. The devil's approach is now direct and clear: "You will not surely die." His tactic ultimately is headed for this conclusion—he will directly attack and contradict what God says. Whenever a person contradicts the obvious and clear teaching of the Bible, you can be sure the devil's wishes are being communicated. It is even possible that the devil is controlling or influencing that person through one of his demons or evil spirits.

Human nature wants to believe that consequences will never be experienced. We do not want to live with that kind of accountability and danger. We prefer to believe that God will be gracious and forgiving no matter what we decide to do. Few of us fear God in terms of the consequences of our actions and decisions. Temptation is always characterized by the belief that we will not suffer the consequences of sinful actions or desires.

Temptation questions God's motives. The devil suggests in this temptation that God's motives are selfish: "For God knows that in the day you eat of it your eyes will be opened, and you will be like God, knowing good and evil" (3:5). He argues that God is trying to keep Adam and Eve from a new and greater understanding and from being like Himself in the sense of what He knows. The devil suggests that it is a good thing to know the difference between, and the nature of, both good and evil. Such has ever been his lie and deception.

Is God trying to keep us from greater knowledge and insights by His restrictions and limitations? Is God really against us, not wanting us to have fun and to enjoy ourselves? Is that really what the Bible teaches? Such arguments are a part of satanic deception—nothing but lies about God and His motives toward the creatures He made.

Temptation promises personal benefits through disobedience. In addition to questioning God's motives, the devil implies that disobedience to what God had said would bring great personal benefits, such as being like God and knowing good and evil. That's how temptation works. It makes us believe that no matter what God has said, doing what you want to do is the only way to real happiness and success.

For example, God says it is wrong to have sexual intercourse with any person except your spouse. The devil's temptations will constantly impress us with the fact that we are missing out on a great deal of sexual pleasure and satisfaction. He will try to convince me that having sex with someone other than my spouse is really quite enjoyable and stimulating. He will try to convince me that there are no losses, only personal benefits. We often compromise because of these temptations and do that which we know God forbids, somehow believing that we will not suffer any consequences, but rather experience renewed happiness and satisfaction.

The devil's methods for tempting us are manifold. He is not limited to one strategy. He will use what seems to be good and right in order to make us disobedient to or dissatisfied with God's instructions and commands.

Temptation appeals to our basic needs and desires. At this point the devil's temptation reaches its intended goal—appealing to what he knows about human nature. At no point do we fall more easily into sinful conduct and practices than when we underestimate the devil's understanding of our weaknesses and human desires. He appeals to what he knows is a part of what we are. We have no choice (in one sense) but to be interested and attracted by what the devil offers because it does reach us where we are, touching our thoughts, feelings, and deepest needs. Eve's basic needs and desires (like those of all of us) fell into three categories: physical, emotional, and intellectual.

Physical—"good for food" ("It will feel good")

Emotional—"pleasant to the eyes" ("It looks good")

Intellectual—"desirable to make one wise" ("It will make me better")

The apostle John gives a similar outline of human desire and need (1 John 2:15-17). He describes the "world" as a system of thinking, a lifestyle without God, a desire that centers in selfish goals and pursuits rather than in the living God. According to these verses, the world consists of three things that affect all of us:

- The lust of the flesh (physical)
- The lust of the eyes (emotional)
- The pride of life (intellectual)

The "pride of life" refers to boasting about one's means of livelihood. It refers to confidence in what we own. It deals with worldly security and the kind of self-esteem our career or occupation brings because of apparent success, that bank account or those investments that give us a measure of importance or worth. All of this kind of thinking is not from God—it is a part of the world's philosophy of life. It leaves God out. Or stated in another way, it has no room for dependence upon God—there is no need.

Adam was not deceived (1 Timothy 2:13-14). He deliberately disobeyed. He accepted what his wife offered to him, knowing that it would violate God's command. Why did Adam disobey when he knew exactly what he was doing? Some say he did it because he loved his wife or at least did not want her to suffer the consequences all alone. He realized she had disobeyed God even though she was deceived by the devil. Perhaps he thought the consequences were not going to be experienced since his wife did not die immediately upon taking the fruit. Although she did not die physically, she did die spiritually. Her subsequent physical death years later was the result of the spiritual death she experienced the day she ate the fruit.

Whatever the logic we may use in trying to discover Adam's motive, the simple truth is that he did it because he wanted to do it. He was responsible for the choice he made. He knew the truth yet disobeyed and sinned against God in spite of it. Many of us sin in exactly the same way. We know the truth of God's Word, yet in spite of what we know we make plans to sin against God.

One of the most serious phases of temptation deals with what we see. The lust of the eyes reminds us all that the door that leads to enticement of our natural tendencies and sinful desires is the eye. What we look at is extremely important in determining whether we yield to temptation.

When David committed adultery with Bathsheba and arranged for the murder of her husband, it is important for us to remember that his downfall began with what he saw. We read in 2 Samuel 11:2 that "he saw a woman bathing, and the woman was very beautiful to behold." Looking at a nude woman taking a bath and taking the time to observe her beautiful body was a part of the process that led to his downfall.

Jesus said in Matthew 5:28 that "whoever looks at a woman to lust for her" has committed adultery with her already in his heart. The process that leads a person to commit actual adultery begins in the mind, and this process is fed by a continual concentration on a particular person with the expressed intent to commit adultery. It is not merely the enjoyment of a woman's physical assets that provides the temptation; it is the desire of the heart to commit adultery with that woman that provides the fuel that fans the flame of temptation and sinful desire.

The Fall
(3:7-24)

⁷Then the eyes of both of them were opened, and they knew that they were naked; and they sewed fig leaves together and made themselves coverings. ⁸And they heard the sound of the LORD God walking in the garden in the cool of the day, and Adam and his wife hid themselves from the presence of the LORD God among the trees of the garden.

⁹Then the LORD God called to Adam and said to him, "Where are you?" ¹⁰So he said, "I heard Your voice in the garden, and I was afraid because I was naked; and I hid myself." ¹¹And He said, "Who told you that you were naked? Have you eaten from the tree of which I commanded you that you should not eat?" ¹²Then the man said, "The woman whom You gave to be with me, she gave me of the tree, and I ate." ¹³And the LORD God said to the woman, "What is this you have done?" And the woman said, "The serpent deceived me, and I ate." ¹⁴So the LORD God said to the serpent:

"Because you have done this,
You are cursed more than all cattle,
And more than every beast of the field;
On your belly you shall go,
And you shall eat dust

All the days of your life.
¹⁵ And I will put enmity
Between you and the woman,
And between your seed and her Seed;
He shall bruise your head,
And you shall bruise His heel."

¹⁶To the woman He said:

"I will greatly multiply your sorrow and your
      conception;
In pain you shall bring forth children;
Your desire shall be for your husband,
And he shall rule over you."

¹⁷Then to Adam He said, "Because you have heeded
the voice of your wife, and have eaten from the tree of
which I commanded you, saying, 'You shall not eat of
it':

"Cursed is the ground for your sake;
In toil you shall eat of it
All the days of your life.
¹⁸ Both thorns and thistles it shall bring forth for
      you,
And you shall eat the herb of the field.

¹⁹ In the sweat of your face you shall eat bread
Till you return to the ground,
For out of it you were taken;
For dust you are,
And to dust you shall return."

²⁰And Adam called his wife's name Eve, because she
was the mother of all living. ²¹Also for Adam and his
wife the LORD God made tunics of skin, and clothed
them.

²²Then the LORD God said, "Behold, the man has
become like one of Us, to know good and evil. And
now, lest he put out his hand and take also of the tree
of life, and eat, and live forever"—²³therefore the
LORD God sent him out of the garden of Eden to till
the ground from which he was taken. ²⁴So He drove

out the man; and He placed cherubim at the east of the garden of Eden, and a flaming sword which turned every way, to guard the way to the tree of life.

Are we fallen creatures? Are children born into this world with sinful natures and dispositions? Is moral depravity a condition of every human heart? Is there evidence in the human experience for the fall of the human race as taught in the Bible?

No teaching of the Bible is resisted any more than the fall and depravity of the human race. Most people want to believe that humanity is inherently good and only becomes evil by the choices we make and the acts we commit. Nothing so urges our need of a Savior as the fact of our moral depravity and utter helplessness in trying to save ourselves. The Bible teaches that we cannot save ourselves (Titus 3:5) and that we are incapable of producing good from God's point of view (Romans 3:10-12). The Bible emphasizes that we are born with a sinful nature (Ephesians 2:1-3) and that it affects everything we do (Isaiah 64:6). Israel's king David said that he was conceived in sin (Psalm 51:5). The Bible clearly teaches that all are sinners by birth and by choice (Romans 3:23; 5:12-14), and that we demonstrated that fact long before we ever knew what was right and wrong in God's law.

The Alternatives Adam and Eve Faced

It should be obvious but let's state it clearly—Adam and Eve had two choices when God commanded them to stay away from the tree of knowledge of good and evil (Genesis 2:17):

1. To obey God and to believe that He knew what was best for them.

2. To disobey God, believing that they had the right to determine their own destiny.

Adam and Eve could have chosen either alternative. They were capable of not sinning as well as sinning against what God had said. It was a moral and spiritual test, a time to decide on the ultimate purpose of all things. Has everything been designed for the purpose of glorifying and honoring God, the Creator? Or is the universe and all that it contains intended to be used by humanity in whatever way we see fit?

The Fall of the Human Race

The Act that Caused the Fall

Adam and Eve were "free" in the sense that they had no sinful nature and desires controlling their actions and decisions. They were "free" to do whatever they wanted with only one restriction—the tree of the knowledge of good and evil. They had no knowledge of the difference between good and evil. Evil was not in their understanding or desires.

So what caused their fall?

Romans 5:14 speaks of Adam's "transgression," a word which means "to step over the line." The line was clearly drawn by God. According to the Bible, it was an outward act of disobedience on the part of Adam that caused the fall of the human race. Adam's sin was also an inward act of his will; he deliberately decided to disobey God. His volitional act led to the outward deed of eating the forbidden fruit. So it is with all of us. The battle begins within our wills, struggling against the known revealed will of God, ultimately leading us to an outward act of disobedience.

**The Awareness the Fall Brought
to Adam and Eve (3:7-8)**

There was a loss of holiness. Before the fall, Adam and Eve enjoyed a relationship with God that was characterized by holiness, a separation from sin. Their awareness that this holy and wonderful relationship with God had changed was immediately evident to them. They knew that something was wrong—"their eyes were opened, and they knew that they were naked." Their nudity previous to the fall was no problem nor was there any sense of shame or embarrassment.

Adam and Eve were not only aware immediately that something was wrong, they tried to hide their shame. Hebrews 4:13 says that all things are "naked" before the eyes of God, the One to Whom we must one day give account of all we have thought, said, and done. Psalm 33:13-15 reminds us of God's knowledge of our sinful ways:

> The LORD looks from heaven;
> He sees all the sons of men.
> From the place of His habitation He looks
> On all the inhabitants of the earth;
> He fashions their hearts individually;
> He considers all their works.

Adam and Eve were immediately aware that their relationship with God had changed and the knowledge they had about themselves was now radically different from the innocence and enjoyment of their pre-fall experience.

There was a loss of fellowship with God. Genesis 3:8 says "Adam and his wife hid themselves *from the presence of the LORD*." Sin does that to all of us. When we lose holiness, we also lose fellowship with the God Who made us. At best, the relationship is strained because of our sin and disobedience.

Psalm 16:11 reminds us that in the presence of the Lord there is "fullness of joy" and at His right hand there are "pleasures forevermore." A terrible loss of fellowship with the living God is experienced when sin enters our lives and disobedience marks our conduct.

The Appeal of God to His Fallen Creatures (3:9-11)

Our God is a God of love and compassion, fully aware of our weaknesses and our need of His help and grace. The beauty of His love and concern is wonderfully portrayed as He seeks out the hiding couple. God's appeal to Adam is based on two things:

1. Reminding him that He desires his fellowship.

2. Reinforcing the basic reason for his fall into sin.

When God said "Where are you?" He graciously reminded Adam that He wanted his fellowship. They had enjoyed a wonderful relationship in the garden before Adam's disobedience. Now, all that had changed. In spite of Adam's sin, God wanted him to know that He still desired his fellowship. The basic reason for Adam's fall was his act of disobedience. The Bible is consistent in presenting this fact to us (1 John 3:4; 1 Timothy 2:14; Ephesians 2:2; Romans 5:14, 19).

The Attempt of Adam and Eve to Justify What They Had Done (3:12-13)

Human nature portrays itself in Genesis 3:12-13 in all too familiar ways! Adam blamed God for giving him the woman ("the woman whom *You* gave to be with me"). Many of us would like to blame God for the choices we have made in life. Whether we realize it or not, much of our bitterness and resentment over the things we have experienced and the consequences we have suffered are directed toward God.

God is certainly to "blame" for making us the way we are. After all, we are made "in His image" and "after His likeness." Our personhood exists because God is a real Person. God knew what we would do if given a choice: We would do whatever we wanted to do. The freedom of our personality has led us into bondage to ourselves and our sinful desires and actions.

However, God is not to be blamed for the choices we make, only for creating us with the power of choice. Adam and Eve chose to obey God until the time of the fall. It was the choice they made that led to their downfall.

Adam also blamed Eve for giving him the fruit. So many people try to blame their environment or some other person for the troubles they have experienced in life. In counseling, there is often an attempt to fix the blame on parental upbringing (or the lack of it) or reactions of spouses. All of us hope to find the answer to our problems in the faults of others. We continue to run away from the obvious—we are guilty and accountable for the decisions and choices we have made in life.

I did not choose my parents, nor was I responsible for the way they trained me and communicated with me. However, I am totally responsible for the way I responded to them and for the choices I made regarding what they told me to do or not to do.

Eve blamed the serpent and explained that she was deceived (something God already knew!), so it could not be her fault. The problem of temptation is serious, but no temptation is responsible for our decisions. We may have been deceived, but that does not excuse our acts of disobedience. It seems that most people who disobey the laws of God are in some way deceived—deceived into believing that those laws are not important nor do they need to be followed. Some may argue that those laws are out-of-date with contemporary society. They insist on the right to do whatever they want, regardless of whatever moral and spiritual laws God may have established for the health and protection of the human race.

The Answer God Gave to the Serpent (3:14-15)

It is somewhat surprising to see that God begins to answer the excuses which Adam and Eve presented by turning to the serpent. The serpent deceived Eve, and for that God will bring a special judgment and present a special plan for the future of mankind.

God will curse the serpent. The words "on your belly you shall go" imply that the serpent did not crawl on his belly through the dust of the ground until this moment. This immediate physical consequence is to be a lasting reminder to all of humanity of what happened in the garden of Eden when Adam and Eve fell into sin. The snake is an appropriate symbol for the devil. Its ways remind us of his ways and the judgment of God upon him.

The final destiny of this "old serpent" (Revelation 12:9), called the Devil and Satan, is the lake of fire where he will be tormented day and night forever and ever (Revelation 20:10). A fitting judgment for this evil one, the destroyer of humanity, the arch-enemy of God and all that is good.

God will cause hostility to exist between the serpent and the woman. The hostility of Satan toward the woman and her seed is obvious throughout history. The "seed" of the woman refers to her descendants, and in Jewish teaching, refers to the Jewish people, who have continually suffered at the hands of Satan. The devil has a special hatred for the Jewish people.

However, the "seed" of the woman in Genesis 3:15 also refers to one particular individual, not a whole group of people. It is referring to the Messiah, Who would come forth from the Jewish people for the salvation of the world. Satan's great hatred and hostility is directed toward the Messiah in particular and all who follow Him in general.

Revelation 12 describes the nation of Israel during the great tribulation period of the end times. Israel is pictured as a woman "clothed with the sun, with the moon under her feet, and on her head a garland of twelve stars." This woman is about to give birth to a male child, and Satan stands ready to "devour her Child as soon as it was born" (12:4). The Child is described in verse 5 as one "who was to rule all nations with a rod of iron," a reference to the Messiah, the "seed of the woman" (cf. Psalm 2).

God will crush the serpent's head through the seed of the woman. The Messiah will crush the head of the serpent. When you crush a snake's head, you kill the snake—he's finished! But notice carefully that the serpent bites the heel of the Messiah—he inflicts a wound that usually is not fatal.

The Fall of the Human Race

Apparently, by the way this passage is written, the moment the serpent delivers a blow to the heel of the Messiah is the same moment in which his head is crushed (cf. 1 John 3:8; Hebrews 2:14-15). The Bible connects the death of Jesus Christ, the Messiah, to the defeat of the devil (John 12:31-33). Satan is a defeated enemy, and his destiny is already settled—he will be in hell forever, not ordering people to shovel coal, but as its chief prisoner!

The Answer God Gave
to the Woman (3:16)

Following God's judgment upon the serpent, the woman is addressed directly and is told there will be two consequences for what she had done: sorrow in childbirth, and subjection to her husband.

The pain the woman would experience in bearing children would be a frequent reminder of the truthfulness of God's Word and the importance of obeying it. The pain would be relieved by the birth of the child, but the difficulty of bearing the child would be a continual reminder of her failure to trust the Lord in the temptation.

A woman's pain in childbearing is used in the Bible as an illustration of the coming tribulation period. First Thessalonians 5:3 tells us there will be a false peace announced by world leaders at the beginning of the tribulation period. But then, "sudden destruction comes upon them, as labor pains upon a pregnant woman."

The subjection of a woman to her husband is a well-established teaching of the Bible, though greatly criticized and resisted by secular society today. The Bible does not teach the subjection of all women to all men; it teaches that a wife is to submit to her own husband (Ephesians 5:22). A marriage and family must have structure in order to function effectively. That is true of all institutions in life. God holds husbands accountable for the decisions they make as leaders of their marriages and families.

First Corinthians 11:3 says that the "head of woman [wife] is man." The Greek word for "man" does not refer to men in general, but may refer specifically to a husband. The Greek word for "woman" is the same as the one for "wife." The context must determine whether it is referring to women in general or a wife in particular. First Corinthians 14:34 tells women (wives) not to speak out in the public services of the church, but to "be

102

submissive, as the law also says." The only passage to which this statement could refer is the one in Genesis 3:16. Wives are not "to have authority over" their husbands (1 Timothy 2:12). And 1 Peter 3:1 tells wives to be submissive to their own husbands even if they (the husbands) are not obedient to God's Word. They are able by their "gentle and quiet spirit" to win their husbands. The submission of wives to their husbands is a continual reminder of the deception and disobedience of Eve.

The Answer God Gave to the Man (3:17-19)

Adam was not deceived; he deliberately disobeyed God's commandment concerning the forbidden fruit. As a part of God's judgment upon him, the ground was cursed. It would no longer be an easy task to acquire food from the ground. Adam would do it "in toil" and "in the sweat of [his] face." The ground itself would be filled with "thorns and thistles." Up to this point, there was no struggle in partaking of the fruit of the garden. It was readily available and required little effort on his part to grow it or cultivate it. Now, things would be different. Romans 8:18-23 speaks of the curse and the desire of the earth to be delivered from it:

> For I consider that the sufferings of this present time are not worthy to be compared with the glory which shall be revealed in us. For the earnest expectation of the creation eagerly waits for the revealing of the sons of God. For the creation was subjected to futility, not willingly, but because of Him who subjected it in hope; because the creation itself also will be delivered from the bondage of corruption into the glorious liberty of the children of God. For we know that the whole creation groans and labors with birth pangs together until now. And not only they, but we also who have the firstfruits of the Spirit, even we ourselves groan within ourselves, eagerly waiting for the adoption, the redemption of our body.

One day the curse will be removed and all creation—including plant life, animal life, and human life—will be delivered from its results. The corruptible will become incorruptible! No more decay, pain, suffering, sorrow, or death—set free forever!

The most serious consequence of all was the pronouncement by God that Adam and his descendants would experience physical death. Genesis 2:7 told us that God formed man "of the dust of the ground." Now God informs Adam that because of his sin and disobedience, he would return to the dust of the ground. Psalm 103:14 reminds us that God's love and compassion is rooted in the fact that He knows what we are really like: "He knows our frame; He remembers that we are dust."

The Action God Takes to Save
Adam and Eve (3:20-24)

Adam expressed confidence in God's promise about the "seed of the woman," as he calls his wife "Eve," which means "the mother of all living." He simply and beautifully accepts God's plan for the salvation and deliverance of the human race from the consequences of sin which he and his wife brought upon us all.

Genesis 3:20-24 brings God's direct involvement into the tragic situation of Adam and Eve's fall and the subsequent depravity of the human race.

He provided special clothing for them. Adam and Eve "sewed fig leaves together and made themselves coverings" (Genesis 3:7). That was their attempt to solve the immediate consequence of their sin. God provided special clothing for them instead of their fig leaves. He used "tunics of skin, and clothed them." These animal skins required animal sacrifices, God's special way of dealing with our sin. The death of an animal was a vivid illustration of how sin must be handled. Since the consequence of sin is death, the animal's death pictured a substitution. Hebrews 10:4 reminds us that the blood of animals could never take away sin—they were only types, or illustrations, pointing to God's supreme sacrifice, His only-begotten Son, Who would die in the place of all who would put their trust in Him. The death of Jesus Christ was a substitutionary sacrifice for our sins.

He protected them from the tree of life. God knew that if Adam and Eve would partake of the fruit of the tree of life, they would be forever separated from His love and salvation. The tree of life represented eternal life and appears in the future heavenly city (Revelation 22:2). Adam and Eve were protected from that tree of life so that they could be saved from their sin and not suffer the eternal consequences of sin in a place God calls "the lake of fire" (Revelation 20:15). Eternal life is a gift of God's grace and love and is found through personal faith and commitment to the Messiah, God's Son, our Savior and Lord Jesus Christ.

Where do you stand? Do you know where you will spend eternity? Do you understand the fall of the human race and the consequences of sin and disobedience against God? Have you acknowledged in your heart that the only way of salvation and deliverance for the human race is through the "seed of the woman," the Messiah? Have you ever made a personal commitment of your life and future to Jesus Christ as your only Lord and Saviour from sin, death, and hell?

God has no other plan!

Chapter 9
The Sanctity of Human Life
(4:1-26)

After Adam and Eve's fall, a result of their disobedience against God's commandment not to eat from the tree of the knowledge of good and evil, a personal tragedy occurs in their family. The consequences of sin often become evident in our marriages and families. Sibling rivalry is taken for granted, and violence in our homes has become a national crisis. It all started long ago.

Genesis 4 records the first murder and describes the beginnings of civilization. Adam and Eve had two sons named Cain and Abel (other sons and daughters came later, Genesis 5:4). The animal skins with which God had clothed Adam and Eve were clear evidence of animal sacrifices which now had become God's way of teaching humanity the need for a ransom or payment for our sin. The death of the animal would substitute for the sin of mankind. Though symbolic, it would represent the faith of the individual who brought the sacrifice. Later, in the law of Moses, great details would be given about these animal sacrifices and their importance.

Cain was a "tiller of the ground," and Abel a "keeper of sheep." Both were required by God to bring an animal sacrifice. The role of raising and providing the animals for such sacrifices was obviously in the hands of Abel. The results of the fall of Adam and Eve would now be seen in the lives of their children. Cain will clearly demonstrate that his heart was not right before God.

The Reason God Did Not Accept Cain's Offering
(4:1-5a)

¹Now Adam knew Eve his wife, and she conceived and bore Cain, and said, "I have gotten a man from the LORD." ²Then she bore again, this time his brother Abel. Now Abel was a keeper of sheep, but Cain was a tiller of the ground. ³And in the process of time it came to pass that Cain brought an offering of the fruit of the ground to the LORD. ⁴Abel also brought of the firstlings of his flock and of their fat. And the LORD respected Abel and his offering, ⁵but He did not respect Cain and his offering.

The New Testament offers a brief commentary about this story: "By faith Abel offered to God a more excellent sacrifice than Cain, through which he obtained witness that he was righteous, God testifying of his gifts; and through it he being dead still speaks" (Hebrews 11:4). It is clear from this verse that Abel's offering was "a more excellent sacrifice" than Cain's. Abel was considered by God to be righteous in what he did. Obviously, Cain was not. The question is, Why? Some possible reasons:

Cain's offering was not an animal sacrifice. We might as well ask whether the principle of sacrifice and worship was already established by God. The fact that both of them "brought an offering" to the Lord implies that they both knew the need to worship the Lord Who made them. Since the sun, moon, and stars (Genesis 1:14) were designed to be "signs and seasons, and for days and years," and the Sabbath day was clearly blessed and sanctified by God (Genesis 2:3), it is quite possible that the day of worship was clearly revealed by God to this first family.

The most powerful argument here would come from Genesis 3:21 where we read that God clothed Adam and Eve with "tunics of skin," implying that sacrifices of animals had taken place.

Cain's offering was the result of his own efforts. It is clear in the Bible that God does not accept the works of our hands as payment for our sins. Our performance is not the key to entering heaven. Salvation is by faith alone, not by the works of humanity. Because of this truth, some have concluded that the basic reason behind God's rejection of Cain's offering was because it represented his own efforts as he would work the ground, whereas Abel's offering was not in that category.

Some rabbinical teaching of the past has contributed to this view. Rabbis argued that Abel was younger yet his occupation was mentioned first in the biblical text. They believe this is done to indicate that Abel's job was a more spiritual pursuit.

Cain's offering was from the ground that was cursed. Cain's offering was "the fruit of the ground." Since the ground was cursed by God (Genesis 3:17), some believe this is the primary reason his offering was not acceptable to God.

Closely related to this view is the possibility that Cain's offering was not accepted because it was inferior to Abel's. Abel brought "the firstlings of his flock and of their fat" (v.4). There is no mention of this in the case of Cain's offering. Is it possible that he brought something less than the "firstborn" or the "firstfruits"? Consider the teaching of Proverbs 3:9-10:

> Honor the LORD with your possessions,
> And with the firstfruits of all your increase;
> So your barns will be filled with plenty,
> And your vats will overflow with new wine.

It is possible that this is the reason Cain's offering was rejected; he did not bring the "firstfruits" (at least there is no mention of it in reference to his offering). The clear reference to Abel's offering as being the "firstlings" presents quite a contrast with Cain's offering.

Cain's attitude was wrong. The simplest point may be more the truth than the other possible views. Verse 4 says "the LORD respected Abel and his offering." He did not respect Cain and his offering (v. 5). The next few verses reveal that Cain's attitude is far from the worship of the Lord. His offering may have been inferior or not the "first" of what he produced, or it may have not been a required animal sacrifice, but behind it all is an attitude that was clearly wrong. In Mark 7:6, Jesus spoke of this problem in worship: "This people honors Me with their lips, but their heart is far from Me."

The Reaction of Cain
(4:5b-8)

**⁵And Cain was very angry, and his countenance fell.
⁶So the LORD said to Cain, "Why are you angry? And**

> why has your countenance fallen? 'If you do well, will
> you not be accepted? And if you do not do well, sin
> lies at the door. And its desire is for you, but you
> should rule over it." ⁸Now Cain talked with Abel his
> brother; and it came to pass, when they were in the
> field, that Cain rose against Abel his brother and killed
> him.

So much for the sanctity of human life! Here, in the very first
family on earth, cold-blooded, premeditated murder takes place.

Cain's anger was immediately displayed. He has a severe attitude
problem. The moment God refused to accept his offering, he
becomes very angry. There has been no mention of such anger
until now. In the garden of Eden where Adam and Eve enjoyed
a special relationship and fellowship with God, there was no
indication of hostile or violent feelings. The results of the fall
are now seen in the life of their son Cain.

Two things are clear: He was unwilling to "do well," and he
was unable to control the sin in his heart. He did not bring the
correct sacrifice and because of that, "sin lies at the door." The
image is that of a lion crouched to leap on you and devour you.
When we disobey God, sin is ready to take us over and consume
us!

Cain's attack on his brother was the expected result. His anger led
to jealousy which led to murder. Hebrews 12:24 refers to the
blood of Jesus Christ shed for our sins and says that it "speaks
better things than that of Abel." The blood of Jesus was shed
voluntarily; He gave His own life for our sins when He died on
the cross. His death and shed blood had a wonderful
purpose—to provide forgiveness for our sins. Abel's blood was
rooted in a senseless, violent act by his brother Cain. It served
no purpose in the behalf of others but rather speaks powerfully
of the depravity of the human heart and the consequences of
the fall of Adam and Eve and the subsequent moral helplessness
of the human race.

In the first epistle of John, the apostle comments on the tragic
story of Cain and Abel:

> In this the children of God and the children of the
> devil are manifest: Whoever does not practice
> righteousness is not of God, nor is he who does not
> love his brother. For this is the message that you

heard from the beginning, that we should love one another, not as Cain who was of the wicked one and murdered his brother. And why did he murder him? Because his works were evil and his brother's righteous. Do not marvel, my brethren, if the world hates you. We know that we have passed from death to life, because we love the brethren. He who does not love his brother abides in death. Whoever hates his brother is a murderer, and you know that no murderer has eternal life abiding in him.

(1 John 3:10-15)

Powerful words of warning! Cain was responding to the deceit and temptation of the devil himself when he allowed his anger to pour out in a jealous rage against his brother.

The Results of Cain's Sin against God
(4:9-24)

God is a God of justice and holiness. Sin must be dealt with justly. Cain's sin of murdering his brother Abel requires the justice of God Himself. Murder is an attack on the Creator Who made humanity in His own image and after His likeness. Human life is sacred because first and foremost, we were made in the image of God.

⁹Then the LORD said to Cain, "Where is Abel your brother?" And he said, "I do not know. Am I my brother's keeper?" ¹⁰And He said, "What have you done? The voice of your brother's blood cries out to Me from the ground. ¹¹So now you are cursed from the earth, which has opened its mouth to receive your brother's blood from your hand. ¹²When you till the ground, it shall no longer yield its strength to you. A fugitive and a vagabond you shall be on the earth." ¹³And Cain said to the LORD, "My punishment is greater than I can bear! ¹⁴Surely You have driven me out this day from the face of the ground; I shall be hidden from Your face; I shall be a fugitive and a vagabond on the earth, and it will happen that anyone who finds me will kill me." ¹⁵And the LORD said to him, "Therefore, whoever kills Cain, vengeance shall be taken on him sevenfold." And the LORD set a mark

on Cain, lest anyone finding him should kill him.

¹⁶Then Cain went out from the presence of the LORD and dwelt in the land of Nod on the east of Eden. ¹⁷And Cain knew his wife, and she conceived and bore Enoch. And he built a city, and called the name of the city after the name of his son—Enoch. ¹⁸To Enoch was born Irad; and Irad begot Mehujael, and Mehujael begot Methushael, and Methushael begot Lamech.

¹⁹Then Lamech took for himself two wives: the name of one was Adah, and the name of the second was Zillah. ²⁰And Adah bore Jabal. He was the father of those who dwell in tents and have livestock. ²¹His brother's name was Jubal. He was the father of all those who play the harp and flute. ²²And as for Zillah, she also bore Tubal-Cain, an instructor of every craftsman in bronze and iron. And the sister of Tubal-Cain was Naamah. ²³Then Lamech said to his wives:

> **"Adah and Zillah, hear my voice;**
> **O wives of Lamech, listen to my speech!**
> **For I have killed a man for wounding me,**
> **Even a young man for hurting me.**
> **²⁴If Cain shall be avenged sevenfold,**
> **Then Lamech seventy-sevenfold."**

Cain's deception could not be hidden from the Lord. Genesis 4:9-15 gives a fascinating insight into human nature and the character of God. One thing is for sure—you can't hide from God! God cursed the serpent in Genesis 3:14, the ground in 3:17, and now Cain in 4:11. The serpent, Adam, and Cain all deserved this judgment of God for acts of sin and disobedience.

Notice the following four things about Cain's attempt to hide from God and to escape His judging hand:

1. He lied (v. 9). His words "I do not know" were a bold lie and that in the presence of God Himself! God's patience and kindness is seen in the way He responded to Cain. His question, "What have you done?" offers Cain the opportunity to repent.

2. He refused to accept responsibility for his brother's welfare (v. 9). It is amazing how many people adopt the philosophy of Cain: "Am I my brother's keeper?" We show little regard or concern for the welfare of others unless we're reasonably sure that personal benefit will accrue to us. The depravity of our hearts is clearly seen in our lack of concern for others. We are more concerned with our rights than our responsibilities.

The world tells us we need to cultivate love for ourselves as a prior condition to loving others. The Bible teaches that we already do love ourselves (Ephesians 5:29) and that our priority is to love others and care for them like we always do for ourselves (Matthew 22:37-39; Philippians 2:3-4).

3. He failed to understand the Lord's omniscience and justice (vv. 10-12). What Cain had done was known to God. All things are known to Him, and we are accountable to Him for what we think, say, and do (Hebrews 4:13). God's judgment was introduced with the words "you are cursed from the earth." What an awesome thought to be cursed by the living God! There were two parts to this curse: one would affect his efforts to till the ground, and the other would affect his desire to have a permanent place he could call "home."

4. He thought the punishment was too great (vv. 13-15). Cain's response—"My punishment is greater than I can bear"—is thought by some scholars to be a question rather than a declarative statement. The word *punishment* could also be translated "iniquity." He could be asking, "Is my iniquity too great to be forgiven?" Cain may be asking God to forgive him for what he had done and not to exercise any penalty, at least not as severe as Cain imagined it would be.

Cain gives two reasons for what he said. He felt the loss of God's presence and protection would be too much, and the result would be that anyone could and probably would kill him because of what he had done. The Lord's response to Cain's appeal is most enlightening. If anyone kills Cain, vengeance would be sevenfold. The Lord set a mark on Cain to insure that no one would kill him. What this mark was, we have no idea. It was simply a guarantee that God would not allow someone to kill Cain. God's judgment would stand, and it was enough.

Cain's departure from the Lord's presence was the most serious consequence. Genesis 4:16 says, "Then Cain went out from the presence of the LORD and dwelt in the land of Nod on the east of Eden." The word *Nod* in Hebrew means "wandering" or "exile." Perhaps the point is that no particular place became his home, but he continued to wander the rest of his life, thus fulfilling God's words: "A fugitive and a vagabond you shall be on the earth."

Cain's descendants were affected by what he had done. Genesis 4:17-24 records Cain's family tree and the results of God's judgment upon him for the murder of his brother Abel.

The common and oft-repeated question "Where did Cain get his wife?" is easily answered by observing Genesis 5:4, for Adam and Eve had both sons and daughters. He obviously married one of his sisters.

It is fascinating to note the name of Cain's first son—Enoch. It means "dedication" or "consecration" or "initiation." It speaks of a new beginning. Cain desires to start over again and build a new life for himself.

Five generations following Cain, Lamech has two wives. The text says "Lamech took for himself two wives." It was not God's original plan (see Matthew 19:4-6). From the act of murder, we now encounter bigamy in the first human civilization on earth. In the same family, murder will occur again as Lamech confesses to killing a young man, although he asserts that it was in self-defense. The words of Lamech are difficult to interpret. He says to his wives, "If Cain shall be avenged sevenfold, then Lamech seventy-sevenfold." Three possible interpretations have been offered for these words:

1. The vengeance refers to the extent of the judgment. This view sees that if Cain is avenged sevenfold, then Lamech would be seventy-sevenfold. As to why his judgment would be more severe is hard to accept in the light of his remarks about killing in self-defense. His act seems to be less wicked than Cain's. Also, the vengeance of Genesis 4:15 is described as being sevenfold on the one who would kill Cain, not on Cain himself.

2. The vengeance refers to God's protection, not His judgment. This view sees the statement as arguing God's protection upon Cain, and then upon Lamech. If God would bring His vengeance upon someone who killed Cain, how much more would he protect Lamech for what he did in self-defense. So Lamech is appealing to God for His protection for killing a young man who had attacked him.

3. The vengeance refers to time. This viewpoint argues that Lamech is the one who kills Cain. The word *sevenfold* in verse 15 refers to seven generations before Cain would be killed. Counting Cain as the first, and the birth of Lamech's children as the seventh generation, Lamech is used by God to bring vengeance upon Cain. Lamech's appeal for "seventy-sevenfold" is asking for a longer period of time before God's judgment would be exercised upon him for killing Cain.

We do know from Genesis 9:6 that God's holy and righteous judgment involves capital punishment for capital crime:

> "Whoever sheds man's blood,
> By man his blood shall be shed;
> For in the image of God
> He made man."

Those who commit murder receive the death penalty under God's law. The sanctity of human life is taught throughout the Bible. Life is precious because we were created by God Himself, and we live because His life has made it possible.

The Realization of God's Plan
(4:25-26)

²⁵And Adam knew his wife again, and she bore a son and named him Seth, "For God has appointed another seed for me instead of Abel, whom Cain killed." ²⁶And as for Seth, to him also a son was born; and he named him Enosh. Then men began to call on the name of the LORD.

The tragic story of the first family is a great moment for all of us to realize the plan of God and to put our trust in Him, not in our ability to handle things ourselves.

It demands our confidence in what God will do. Verse 25 records the faith and confidence of Eve in the plan of the Lord. She knew about God's promise to her (Genesis 3:15) that her Seed would crush the serpent and bring the victory they so desperately needed. Her statement, "For God has appointed another seed for me instead of Abel," reveals her confidence in the Lord and His plan for her and the whole human race.

It demonstrates our need to call upon the name of the Lord. The last statement of Genesis 4 is, "Then men began to call on the name of the LORD." The tragic events of chapter 4 brought men and women to their knees. Does it do the same for you?

The only answer to the depravity and sin of our hearts is to call upon the name of the Lord (Romans 10:13, Acts 2:21). Acts 4:12 states it quite clearly: "Nor is there salvation in any other, for there is no other name under heaven given among men by which we must be saved."

Chapter 10

The Beginning of Civilization

(5:1-32)

Civilization involves people. People develop culture, customs, laws, institutions, cities, economies, and so on. The first civilization that developed from Adam and Eve was mentioned in Genesis 4 in the family of Cain. Cities were built and trades were developed, including animal husbandry (v. 20), musical instruments (v. 21), and manufacturing of bronze and iron (v. 22).

Cain's family was rooted in tragedy and sin. Cain was a vagabond and a fugitive on the earth. A degree of sensitivity to the Lord is seen in the remarks of his descendant Lamech (4:24), but the Bible seems to indicate that those who followed the Lord and called upon His name were found in the line of Seth, the son given to Adam and Eve instead of Abel. It is through the line of Seth that the future Messiah will come who will crush the head of the serpent (3:15).

The genealogical list of Genesis 5 offers interesting insights into the character and design of God Himself. It reveals some wonderful things about God and His work in the course of human history.

The Personality of God Is Revealed
(5:1-2)

¹**This is the book of the genealogy of Adam. In the day that God created man, He made him in the likeness of God. ²He created them male and female, and blessed them and called them Mankind in the day they were created.**

Three times we are told that God created the human race and once we are told He made them. The Bible never allows us to escape its opening words "In the beginning God created." Without a Creator, human history is indeed a mystery. Trying to discover origins without the Originator is like looking at a beautiful watch and wondering how all the intricate pieces happened to fall together to make it work so well!

Genesis 1:26-27 told us that man and woman were both created in the image of God and after His likeness. There is something of God Himself in each of us! Interestingly, Genesis 5:3 states that Adam "begot a son in his own likeness, after his image." Seth was like Adam in some way, even though they probably did not have identical physical features.

It is the personality of God that is involved in the statement "in His image . . . after His likeness." Because God thinks, we are capable of rational thought; because God has emotions, we are creatures of great feeling and desire; because God's will governs His actions, we also have the ability to make volitional choices. That which continues to be seen throughout the development of the human race is the fact of personality, existing within each person conceived and born into the human race.

Being created in God's image is a reason not to lie to one another. Colossians 3:9-10 says: "Do not lie to one another, since you have put off the old man with his deeds, and have put on the new man who is renewed in knowledge according to the image of Him who created him."

Those who become believers in Jesus Christ are exhorted to stop lying to one another. It is our natural tendency to deceive others, to make them think we are better than we are, or not as bad we are. Our new relationship to Jesus Christ has settled the issues of depravity and deceit, and we are now taught to live openly and honestly before all men. The reason? We were created in the image of God, and when we become believers, that image is "renewed" or made alive in a way that we could not experience before our conversion. Lying to one another is an attack upon the personality of us all. We were made in the image of God and we deserve better.

Being created in God's image is a reason not to curse another person. James 3:8-10 emphasizes this responsibility:

But no man can tame the tongue. It is an unruly evil,

full of deadly poison. With it we bless our God and Father, and with it we curse men, who have been made in the similitude of God. Out of the same mouth proceed blessing and cursing. My brethren, these things ought not to be so.

The way we treat other people is remarkable. Our disdain for an individual's worth and importance is clear by the way we attack, criticize, slander, and curse. People are made in the image of God, and we have no right to attack their character and personality. Yes, we must deal with acts of wrongdoing, but to judge any person as being worthless because of circumstances, events, or acts of antisocial behavior (no matter how serious their depravity or disability) is a clear violation of the Bible's teaching. Every person has worth because every person has been made in the image of God and after His likeness.

The Plan of God Is Revealed
(5:2-20)

The Propagation of Mankind

It is a simple statement, but contains a tremendous point: God "blessed them," this first human civilization. Genesis 1:28 tells us what that blessing involves: "Be fruitful and multiply; fill the earth and subdue it; have dominion over the fish of the sea, over the birds of the air, and over every living thing that moves on the earth." The concept that the first humans on this planet were victims of a violent animal world over which they had no control is simply not taught in the Bible. A part of the blessing of God was the command to "have dominion over" the animal world.

The primary point behind the blessing of God upon the human race is the propagation of that race. The command "be fruitful and multiply" is God's plan. He wants us to have children, to multiply. Consider His words to Noah following the devastation of the flood (Genesis 9:1; cf. 9:7): "So God blessed Noah and his sons, and said to them: 'Be fruitful and multiply, and fill the earth.' " No concern over population control. God's blessing involves lots of people, and the planet filled with them! In simple words, God's plan involves people. May we

119

lose sight of that fact while we try to live in a culture dominated by material things.

The Death of Mankind

God's blessing involves the propagation of the human race—that is His plan. However, a little phrase that occurs throughout Genesis 5—"and he died"—reveals that God's plan also includes the death of humanity as well as its development. Death is the consequence of Adam's sin (Genesis 2:17, 3:19, Romans 6:23). Romans 5:12 tells us, "through one man sin entered the world, and death through sin, and thus death spread to all men, because all sinned." Take a moment and reflect on the following list of names:

Adam lived 930 years, and he died

Seth (912 years) . . . and he died

Enosh (905 years) . . . and he died

Cainan (910 years) . . . and he died

Mahalaleel (895 years) . . . and he died

Jared (962 years) . . . and he died

Methuselah (969 years) . . . and he died

Lamech (777 years) . . . and he died

With the exception of Enoch, each man's death is recorded. The phrase "and he died" becomes a reminder of the consequences of Adam and Eve's fall.

The good news of the gospel of Jesus Christ is proclaimed by Jesus Himself:

Most assuredly, I say to you, he who hears My word and believes in Him who sent Me has everlasting life, and shall not come into judgment, but has passed from death into life. (John 5:24)

I am the resurrection and the life. He who believes in Me, though he may die, he shall live. And whoever lives and believes in Me shall never die. (John 11:25-26)

The phrase "and he died" reveals the plan of God as to the consequences of sin and disobedience. Yet we can pass from death into life by putting our faith and trust in Jesus Christ as our only Lord and Savior from sin, death, and hell.

The Longevity of Early Mankind

The remarkable thing is that seven of the eight men listed above lived more than eight hundred years. Yet, if our math is correct in following this genealogical table, from the creation of Adam to the birth of Noah's sons would be only 1556 years. Adam would have been a contemporary of Lamech, the father of Noah, for forty-six years.

This longevity, plus the fact that each man "had sons and daughters," argues for a vast population by the time of Noah and the flood. Assuming that the sons and daughters also had children, and assuming that the plurals "sons" and "daughters" argues for at least four children in each case, that would result in a tremendous population by the time of the flood. Also, observe the age at which the first child is born to these men:

Adam—130 years	Jared—162 years
Seth—105 years	Enoch—65 years
Enosh—90 years	Methuselah—187 years
Cainan—70 years	Lamech—182 years
Mahalaleel—65 years	

Is it possible that their ability to bear children continued throughout their lifetime? If that is so, then the population of the world would have been into the millions by the time of the flood.

How do we explain their longevity? Lifespans after the flood drop dramatically from those before the flood. This has caused a number of scientists to believe that the atmospheric conditions before the flood were radically different from those after the flood. The environment before the flood was something like a tropical greenhouse, according to some scientists, due to a vapor canopy which they believe existed around the earth. This canopy collapsed at the time of the flood, causing the enormous amount of water on the entire planet.

It may be that no rainfall occurred before the flood. According to the Bible, God watered the ground by bringing moisture up from the earth itself (Genesis 2:6). It is quite possible that the environment was a contributing factor to the longevity of people before the flood.

Another possibility is that the longevity deals with the effects of sin and the fall of the human race. This view argues that sin took time to do its damage on the physical part of humanity.

The Bible does not tell us why or how men lived so long before the flood, but this longevity does argue for a vast population, possibly millions of people, at the time of the flood.

The Purpose of God Is Revealed
(5:21-24)

²¹**Enoch lived sixty-five years, and begot Methuselah.** ²²**After he begot Methuselah, Enoch walked with God three hundred years, and begot sons and daughters.** ²³**So all the days of Enoch were three hundred and sixty-five years. ²⁴And Enoch walked with God; and he was not, for God took him.**

The story of Enoch and the way he was taken by God out of this world is indeed remarkable! God's purpose for the human race which He created is to have them "walk with" Him. God enjoyed that special relationship with Adam and Eve in the garden of Eden (3:8). We are now confronted with a man, early in human history, who "walked with God." Apparently he began this special relationship with God after the birth of his first son, Methuselah.

In the New Testament we have some additional information about this unusual man, Enoch, and his special relationship with God. Hebrews 11:5-6 comments:

> By faith Enoch was translated so that he did not see death, "and was not found because God had translated him"; for before his translation he had this testimony, that he pleased God. But without faith it is impossible to please Him, for he who comes to God must believe that He is, and that He is a rewarder of those who diligently seek Him.

God's special purpose for the human race is seen in the life of Enoch, a man who "walked with God." According to these verses, that lifestyle was characterized by three things: a desire to please God, faith in God and what He can do, and diligence in seeking God. It would be difficult to imagine a more powerful statement regarding the purpose of humanity.

Obviously, it is God-centered, not man-centered. Ultimate reality and purpose in life must be rooted in the God Who made us and the One to Whom we must one day give account.

A second passage in the New Testament sheds some light on this man Enoch. Jude 14-15 states:

> Now Enoch, the seventh from Adam, prophesied about these men also, saying, "Behold, the Lord comes with ten thousands of His saints, to execute judgment on all, to convict all who are ungodly among them of all their ungodly deeds which they have committed in an ungodly way, and of all the harsh things which ungodly sinners have spoken against Him."

We are told that Enoch "prophesied" and warned his generation about the coming judgment of God upon the ungodly sinners of his day. That was undoubtedly a reference to the coming worldwide flood that arrived in Noah's time. Genesis 5 indicates that Enoch walked with God for three hundred years, following the birth of his son Methuselah, the oldest man who ever lived (969 years).

Enoch proclaimed the message of coming judgment to his generation, and instead of following their ungodly practices, he began to walk with God and fulfill the original purpose of God for humanity. God was so pleased with his commitment that a remarkable event occurred, putting God's stamp of approval upon the lifestyle and commitment of this man Enoch. The Bible says that "he was not, for God took him."

One day he is living on this planet, and the next day he is taken away by God Himself! It is quite similar to the grand and glorious event that the Bible teaches will occur one day when believers will suddenly disappear from this planet and be raptured (taken away) into the presence of the Lord, even though they have not as yet died. This wonderful event is foretold in 1 Thessalonians 4:16-17:

> For the Lord Himself will descend from heaven with a shout, with the voice of an archangel, and with the trumpet of God. And the dead in Christ will rise first. Then we who are alive and remain shall be caught up together with them in the clouds to meet the Lord in the air. And thus we shall always be with the Lord.

This translation of believers to heaven before they die is quite similar to what happened to Enoch. God simply took him out of this world while he was yet alive. He thus becomes an example to all believers as to what a godly lifestyle is all about. We learn powerfully from the life of Enoch what it means to "walk with God." It involves a life dedicated to pleasing God, believing in Him and what He can do, and diligently seeking Him as a daily habit of life.

The Patience of God Is Revealed
(5:28-32)

28Lamech lived one hundred and eighty-two years, and begot a son. 29And he called his name Noah, saying, "This one will comfort us concerning our work and the toil of our hands, because of the ground which the LORD has cursed." 30After he begot Noah, Lamech lived five hundred and ninety-five years, and begot sons and daughters. 31So all the days of Lamech were seven hundred and seventy-seven years; and he died.

32And Noah was five hundred years old, and Noah begot Shem, Ham, and Japheth.

In the New Testament, Hebrews 11:7 comments on the faith of Noah and explains that God warned him of the things which Enoch had prophesied years earlier: "By faith Noah, being divinely warned of things not yet seen, moved with godly fear, prepared an ark for the saving of his household, by which he condemned the world and became heir of the righteousness which is according to faith." First Peter 3:20 speaks of the "longsuffering [patience] of God" during the days of Noah while the ark was being prepared. God's patience with the ungodliness and wickedness of that pre-flood civilization was running out, necessitating holy and just punishment.

It is enlightening to read that Noah "walked with God" (Genesis 6:9), the same phrase used of Enoch. God's purpose is that humanity live in close fellowship and relationship with Him. His patience endures man's sin and disobedience, but not forever. Psalm 103:8-14 is encouraging to all of us who try the patience of God and wonder about His delays:

The LORD is merciful and gracious,
Slow to anger, and abounding in mercy.
He will not always strive with us,
Nor will He keep His anger forever.
He has not dealt with us according to our sins,
Nor punished us according to our iniquities.

For as the heavens are high above the earth,
So great is His mercy toward those who fear Him;
As far as the east is from the west,
So far has He removed our transgressions from us.
As a father pities his children,

So the LORD pities those who fear Him.
For He knows our frame;
He remembers that we are dust.

God is patient and slow to anger—"He will not always strive with us, nor will He keep His anger forever." What a statement! But the fact that God is patient does not mean He will allow sin to go unpunished. Finally, in the days of Noah, that first human civilization learned that God is a God of holiness and justice as well as love and mercy. In the midst of a wicked and terrible culture, Enoch and Noah were refreshing examples of men who knew the meaning of life and the importance of "walking with God."

The genealogical table of the first human civilization reveals amazing things about God as well as the development of the people of that pre-flood planet. Millions of people spread across the earth due to the longevity and productivity of these ancient people, but the sad truth, which we shall explore in depth in the next chapter, is that their hearts were far from God. The fall and depravity of the human race had reached monstrous proportions, requiring the intervention and judgment of Almighty God.

God's personality, plan, purpose, and patience are revealed in Genesis 5. Exactly where do you find yourself in relation to these great truths? Do you understand that you are a person created in God's image? Do you see or understand His plan? Have you come to grips with the ultimate purpose and meaning of human life? What place does God hold in your priorities, commitments, and decisions?

God's judgment upon that pre-flood society was inevitable. To all those who refuse to acknowledge the God Who made them and turn their backs on the only One Who can save them from their own sin and depravity, the only thing that remains is the awesome reality of God's judgment.

Pay day some day!

Chapter 11

Human Depravity and Divine Judgment

(6:1-13)

From the beauty of the garden of Eden to the world of Noah's day is no testimony to evolution, but to devolution. Mankind does not get better, but worse. From the fall of Adam and Eve to the time of Noah, the human race had tried the patience of God and was ripe for judgment.

The Causes Behind the Wickedness of Men
(6:1-4)

¹Now it came to pass, when men began to multiply on the face of the earth, and daughters were born to them, ²that the sons of God saw the daughters of men, that they were beautiful; and they took wives for themselves of all whom they chose. ³And the LORD said, "My Spirit shall not strive with man forever, for he is indeed flesh; yet his days shall be one hundred and twenty years." ⁴There were giants on the earth in those days, and also afterward, when the sons of God came in to the daughters of men and they bore children to them. Those were the mighty men who were of old, men of renown.

The multiplication of people. It is quite possible that the pre-flood population numbered in the millions. Whenever people multiply, problems inevitably will follow. Because the human race had fallen, the potential for serious problems was within the heart of every person born into that civilization. That is still true today. More people, more problems.

The marriages that took place. The Bible tells us that the "sons of God" married the "daughters of men," and the result was "giants on the earth in those days." This difficult passage has continued to fascinate students of the Bible, and there are various interpretations of it. The three basic questions to be answered are: Who are the "sons of God"? Who are the "daughters of men"? Who are the "giants on the earth"?

1. Who are the "sons of God"? The word for "God" (*elohim*) in Hebrew is a plural form. It can also be translated "gods." The word is used in the Bible to refer to the rulers or judges of Israel because of the authority they received from God Himself. One view of the phrase "sons of God" is that it should read "sons of the gods," referring to children of the rulers who because of the abuse of power and position took whomever they wanted to be their wives, whether or not they were already married to someone else. Genesis 6:2 says, "they took wives for themselves of all whom they chose." The way it is stated implies a selfish, arrogant, and unethical practice.

A second view of the "sons of God" is that it refers to the godly line of Seth. Genesis 4:25-26 makes it clear that God "appointed another seed" for Adam and Eve to replace Abel, who was killed by Cain. This viewpoint assumes that those in the line of Seth were believers while those in the line of Cain were unbelievers. This view interprets the problems and wickedness of the pre-flood society to the marriage of believers with unbelievers.

A third view is that the "sons of God" refers to angels. The phrase is used that way elsewhere in the Bible. Job 1:6 and 2:1 speak of "the sons of God" who came to present themselves before the Lord. Interestingly, Satan was one of them. Job 38:7 speaks of the joy of angels at the time of creation as they "shouted for joy." It calls them "sons of God."

Angels are spirits (Hebrews 1:14), and there are good angels as well as evil angels. Evil angels or spirits are also called demons in the Bible. The Bible refers to the "devil and his angels" (Revelation 12:7-9) and indicates that evil spirits can inhabit the bodies of human beings (Mark 1:23, 32-34; 5:2).

Two passages in the New Testament are used to support this view that the "sons of God" in Genesis 6 are actually angels. Second Peter 2:4-6 says:

> For if God did not spare the angels who sinned, but
> cast them down to hell and delivered them into chains

> of darkness, to be reserved for judgment; and did not spare the ancient world, but saved Noah, one of eight people, a preacher of righteousness, bringing in the flood on the world of the ungodly; and turning the cities of Sodom and Gomorrah into ashes, condemned them to destruction, making them an example to those who afterward would live ungodly.

This passage connects sinful angels and the "ancient world" of Noah's day, and the cities of Sodom and Gomorrah. Jude 6-7 makes a similar connection:

> And the angels who did not keep their proper domain, but left their own habitation, He has reserved in everlasting chains under darkness for the judgment of the great day; as Sodom and Gomorrah, and the cities around them in a similar manner to these, having given themselves over to sexual immorality and gone after strange flesh, are set forth as an example, suffering the vengeance of eternal fire.

These angels did the following: (1) They left their own habitation; (2) they gave themselves over to sexual immorality; and (3) they went after strange flesh.

On the basis of these statements, many Bible teachers and scholars have interpreted the phrase "the sons of God" to be angels, spirits who inhabited the physical bodies of those on earth and committed acts of sexual immorality that brought the judgment of God upon that first civilization.

2. Who are the "daughters of men"? Two basic views are proposed for this phrase. One is that it is a reference to unbelievers. This view connects with the argument that the "sons of God" refers to the believers of the godly line of Seth. A second view is that the "daughters of men" simply refers to women in general.

3. Who are the "giants on the earth"? The Hebrew term *nephilim* is used in Numbers 13:33 to refer to those of great physical stature: "There we saw the giants (the descendants of Anak came from the giants); and we were like grasshoppers in our own sight, and so we were in their sight." It is possible that the "giants on the earth" were simply those of great physical stature. The word also appears in the passage in Genesis 10:8-9 where Nimrod is described as a "mighty one on the earth."

Genesis 6:4 says that the children that were born to the union of the "sons of God" and the "daughters of men" were "the mighty men who were of old, men of renown." Perhaps the point deals with their power and influence rather than their physical size. They were giants in the sense of their wickedness and violence.

It is difficult to be dogmatic on the interpretation of these verses. Whatever the meaning of the terms, the basic point of the passage in Genesis 6 is that the result was a violent and wicked civilization that deserved the judgment of God.

The message from the Lord. The Lord made the following evaluation of the pre-flood civilization: "My Spirit shall not strive with man forever, for he is indeed flesh; yet his days shall be one hundred and twenty years." This statement has been variously interpreted. Some say that the words "my spirit" actually refer to the spirit of man, which came from God and gave man life (Genesis 2:7). The meaning then would be that the longevity of man described in Genesis 5 would no longer be available. God would now limit man's existence to a maximum of 120 years. After the flood there appears to be a great reduction in man's lifespan upon the earth.

A second view is that the words "My Spirit" refer to the Holy Spirit of God. The verse then speaks of the Spirit's process of conviction and the longsuffering of God. Each person is given opportunity to turn to the Lord, and a warning is given in this passage that the day of opportunity, rooted in God's patience, will not last forever.

The statement about man's days being "one hundred and twenty years" might refer to the time before the flood would come. Since the flood came in the six hundredth year of Noah's life (Genesis 7:11), then this warning came from God before his three sons were born (cf. Genesis 5:32). Hebrews 11:7 says:

> By faith Noah, being divinely warned of things not yet seen, moved with godly fear, prepared an ark for the saving of his household, by which he condemned the world and became heir of the righteousness which is according to faith.

This verse might imply that it took Noah 120 years to build the ark. First Peter 3:20 describes the "longsuffering of God" that "waited in the days of Noah, while the ark was being prepared." And 2 Peter 2:5 states that Noah was "a preacher of righteousness." Perhaps Noah preached for 120 years as he was building the ark, warning the pre-flood civilization of the coming judgment of God.

The Concern of the Lord Himself
(6:5-7)

⁵Then the LORD saw that the wickedness of man was great in the earth, and that every intent of the thoughts of his heart was only evil continually. ⁶And the LORD was sorry that He had made man on the earth, and He was grieved in His heart. ⁷So the LORD said, "I will destroy man whom I have created from the face of the earth, both man and beast, creeping thing and birds of the air, for I am sorry that I have made them."

The Hebrew word for "was sorry" (*nacham*) speaks of regret and repentance and also of compassion and comfort. It is used some thirty times in the Bible with God as its subject. God changes His mind or His plan or intention, always in accord with His righteous purposes.

The statement appears to be more for our benefit than for His. God always knows what He is going to do before it happens. Human history has already occurred in the mind and plan of God. All changes are only those seen from our point of view, not His. Malachi 3:6 and Hebrews 6:17-18 both speak of the immutability of God, the fact that He does not change.

Our passage in Genesis 6 speaks not only of God being sorry that He had made mankind, but that He was personally "grieved."

The Reason for God's Concern

There are several possible viewpoints in dealing with the sorrow and grief of God over the human civilization He created:

He is sad because these sinners are His handiwork; He is grieved at what they have become. A similar incident is found in 1 Samuel 15:11, where God displays strong emotion in giving expression to His sadness over Saul's failure as king: "I greatly regret that I have set up Saul as king, for he has turned back from following

Me, and has not performed My commandments."

He is consoled by the fact that His judgment is deserved by them. Instead of translating that the Lord "was sorry," this view utilizes the meaning "to console." God is comforted in His grief in that His righteous and holy character will be vindicated by the judgment He will bring upon a society that deserves to be punished.

He is grieved because He does not desire the death of the wicked but that they should repent and live. This view is more plausible than the previous one and is certainly possible. Ezekiel 18:23 and 32 argue for this perspective of God's sorrow over the pre-flood civilization that fell into deep depravity and corruption: " 'Do I have any pleasure at all that the wicked should die?' says the Lord GOD, 'and not that he should turn from his ways and live? . . . For I have no pleasure in the death of one who dies,' says the Lord GOD. Therefore turn and live!' "

He is grieved because the execution of His judgment is always displeasing to Him. This view is also very possible. God's grief could be expressed because God's knowledge of His judgment is never a happy thought to Him. There is a closeness between this view and the one previously mentioned. It appeals to most of us because we cannot imagine God's character in any other way. Lamentations 3:31-33 expresses this thought:

> For the Lord will not cast off forever.
> Though He causes grief,
> Yet He will show compassion
> According to the multitude of His mercies.
> For He does not afflict willingly,
> Nor grieve the children of men.

God is not delighted with the necessity of exercising His judgment. This could very well be the reason for His grief in making mankind and now knowing that their wickedness requires His judgment.

Due to the wickedness of man, God changes His plans for the blessing and propagation of the human race. This seems to be the most natural interpretation of the passage. Whatever blessing God had bestowed upon the human race, He now changes His plan. The fact is, He knew all along what He was going to do. If mankind would walk with God and live in close fellowship with

Him, then God's unchanging character would continue to bless the human race. If people decide to be ungodly in their ways and fill the earth with violence and wickedness, then the unchanging just and holy character of God demands that judgment take place.

God is always consistent with His own nature and character. The apparent changes in God's plans are based on the performance of the people He created, and none of their thoughts or acts are hidden from His knowledge.

God indicates a change in what He was going to do in the case of the children of Israel and the golden calf at Mount Sinai. Exodus 32:14 states, "So the LORD relented from the harm which He said He would do to His people." This came in response to the plea and intercession of Moses.

The same thing can be seen in God's response to the judgment imposed upon the children of Israel because of David's sin in numbering them contrary to God's desires. In 2 Samuel 24:16 we read that "the LORD relented from the destruction, and said to the angel who was destroying the people, 'It is enough; now restrain Your hand.' "

The Result of God's Concern

Genesis 6:7 quotes the Lord's verdict: "I will destroy man whom I have created from the face of the earth, both man and beast, creeping thing and birds of the air, for I am sorry that I have made them." The only thing God could do in the light of the terrible wickedness of the pre-flood human civilization was to destroy them. God's evaluation was that of Psalm 14:1-3:

> The fool has said in his heart,
> "There is no God."
> They are corrupt,
> They have done abominable works,
> There is none who does good.
>
> The LORD looks down from heaven upon the children
>   of men,
> To see if there are any who understand, who seek God.
> They have all turned aside,
> They have together become corrupt;

> There is none who does good,
> No, not one.

We all deserve the judgment of God. It is the good news of the gospel that says there is "no condemnation to those who are in Christ Jesus" (Romans 8:1). God manifests His righteous character in His judgment. The world of Noah's day deserved God's judgment, and so do we today. Yet, because of faith in Jesus Christ, we who deserve judgment are forgiven and delivered because He bore our judgment on the cross.

What a wonderful message!

The Contrast One Man Displayed
(6:8-10)

⁸But Noah found grace in the eyes of the LORD.

⁹This is the genealogy of Noah. Noah was a just man, perfect in his generations. Noah walked with God. ¹⁰And Noah begot three sons: Shem, Ham, and Japheth.

Although the wickedness of man was great in the earth (6:5) there was one man who walked with God. No matter how bad our surroundings may be, the Bible makes it clear that we can be victorious and not succumb to the temptations and sinful practices of this world.

The Response of the Lord

Noah "found grace in the eyes of the LORD." This is the first mention of one of the most beautiful words in the Bible—*grace*. Grace gives us what we do not deserve and sustains us through all of life. Were it not for God's grace, Noah would not have been spared.

Exodus 33:12-17 tells us that Moses likewise found grace in the eyes of the Lord because he pled for God's pardon and forgiveness for the sin of the people of Israel (Exodus 34:9). Psalm 84:11 describes our gracious God:

> For the LORD God is a sun and shield;
> The LORD will give grace and glory;
> No good thing will He withhold
> From those who walk uprightly.

The Reasons behind God's Response

Grace is given by God apart from human efforts (Ephesians 2:9-10). From the human side, grace is a special resource from God based on man's walk with God.

Noah is described as a "just man, perfect in his generations," and elsewhere as "a preacher of righteousness" (2 Peter 2:5). He stood for what is right in the midst of a sinful culture. His character was untainted by manipulation, hypocrisy, and hidden agendas. Genesis 6:9 also says that he "walked with God" like Enoch before him (Genesis 5:24).

Yet 1 Peter 3:20 makes it clear that the "longsuffering of God" was behind the salvation of Noah and his family. As commendable as Noah's conduct, character, and commitment were, in the final analysis it was God's compassion that saved him. "Through the Lord's mercies we are not consumed, because His compassions fail not" (Lamentations 3:22).

The Inevitable Consequence
(6:11-13)

¹¹The earth also was corrupt before God, and the earth was filled with violence. ¹²So God looked upon the earth, and indeed it was corrupt; for all flesh had corrupted their way on the earth. ¹³And God said to Noah, "The end of all flesh has come before Me, for the earth is filled with violence through them; and behold, I will destroy them with the earth."

Basic Reasons for God's Judgment

Corruption. The Hebrew word translated "corrupt" means "to decay." It comes to mean "to ruin," as a result of a decaying process. Ezekiel 23:11 uses the word in a context filled with immorality. Sexual immorality makes a society corrupt before God and deserving of His judgment. That was clearly the cause of the judgment of Sodom and Gomorrah (Jude 6-7). To engage in idolatry is also to act corruptly (Deuteronomy 4:16, 25) and deserves the judgment of God (Deuteronomy 31:29). The word is also used of lying and deceit in Daniel 2:9.

This corruption that permeated the first human civilization was done "before God." If the word *God* is translated "gods," then the point would be that this corruption was done in the presence of the rulers and leaders of the pre-flood society. Some take the phrase "before God" to mean that it was only known to God and that most of society was not aware of how bad things really were. Perhaps the best view of the phrase "before God" is that the corruption was very public and now deserves the judgment and intervention of God.

Violence. The word for "violence" is used of robbery, taking wives by force, and murder. The entire social fabric had disintegrated and human life was no longer sacred and respected. Isaiah 59:6-8 also speaks of terrible violence deserving the judgment of God:

> Their webs will not become garments,
> Nor will they cover themselves with their works;
> Their works are works of iniquity,
> And the act of violence is in their hands.
> Their feet run to evil,
> And they make haste to shed innocent blood;
> Their thoughts are thoughts of iniquity;
> Wasting and destruction are in their paths.
> The way of peace they have not known,
> And there is no justice in their ways;
> They have made themselves crooked paths;
> Whoever takes that way shall not know peace.

What a commentary on a violent society! The whole world (with the exception of eight people) is filled with sexual immorality, idolatry, lying and deceitful practices, theft, rape, and murder. What a mess! The only solution is God's judgment—the whole world destined for destruction.

The pre-flood civilization sounds remarkably similar to our own. God will never destroy the world again with a flood, but He will destroy it again. The next time it will be by fire. The Bible teaches that "the heavens will pass away with a great noise, and the elements will melt with fervent heat; both the earth and the works that are in it will be burned up" (2 Peter 3:10).

The good news is that a new physical universe will be designed by God where "righteousness dwells" (2 Peter 3:13). All believers in God's plan of salvation through His Son, the Messiah, will be a part of that new world. God's kingdom will be set up on earth and believers will reign with our Lord and Savior Jesus Christ, the One Who is called "KING OF KINGS, AND LORD OF LORDS" (Revelation 19:16)!

Global catastrophe came upon the first human civilization and it will once again come upon this planet. We are again ripe for the judgment of God. Have you made your commitment to Jesus Christ? Time is running out!

Chapter 12
Global Catastrophe
(6:14-9:19)

The story of human life and history is uniquely connected to the biblical account of the flood. Without it, a discussion of origins is not complete. The Bible teaches that God destroyed the world with a flood. It also connects that event with future events. Yet the description of the flood and the survival of eight people in the ark are denied by many scientists. They treat the story of the flood as one of many ancient myths whose only historical accuracy is the fact that local floods occurred at various times in ancient history as they do today. The flood story in the book of Genesis is one of the primary reasons why the Bible is not accepted as reliable and accurate.

There are four basic issues that must be considered when dealing with the story of the flood in the book of Genesis:

The geological issue—was it a universal flood that destroyed the entire planet?

The biological issue—could the animals all fit into the ark and survive?

The historical issue—is there any evidence for such a flood outside of the Bible's account?

The spiritual issue—why did God bring such a disaster upon the earth?

The account of the flood begins in Genesis 6:14 with the instructions for building the ark and continues through chapter 9 with a promise from God that He will never again destroy the entire planet with a flood. He makes a covenant with Noah and his sons that has the rainbow as its sign. The rainbow is a reminder that God's promise stands, and He will be faithful to it.

The Geological Issue

Did a flood occur that covered the entire earth? Is that a geological possibility? Does the Bible actually teach that such a flood did happen or does it refer only to a local event in the Mesopotamian valley? Let's carefully look at what the Bible says before we make a judgment. We may not agree with the Bible's teaching, but we must first understand what it is saying before we pass judgment. Bible teachers and scientists have disagreed sharply over the biblical presentation.

The depth of the flood waters. One of the crucial questions regarding the geological possibility of a universal flood deals with the depth of the flood waters. Genesis 6:17 makes it clear that God's judgment was to bring "the flood of waters on the earth, to destroy from under heaven all flesh in which is the breath of life; and everything that is on the earth shall die." It is clear from this verse that God intended it to be a global catastrophe that would destroy "all flesh," and it clearly states the location as "on the earth."

Genesis 7:10 states that "the waters of the flood were on the earth." Genesis 7:17-20 describes the depth of these waters on the earth:

> **17Now the flood was on the earth forty days. The waters increased and lifted up the ark, and it rose high above the earth. 18The waters prevailed and greatly increased on the earth, and the ark moved about on the surface of the waters. 19And the waters prevailed exceedingly on the earth, and all the high hills under the whole heaven were covered. 20The waters prevailed fifteen cubits upward, and the mountains were covered.**

The language in these verses implies that the flood waters covered the entire planet. The text directly states that "all the high hills under the whole heaven were covered," and that "the mountains were covered." We are told that the water covered the mountains and high hills by fifteen cubits or over twenty-two feet.

The duration of the flood. In addition to statements about the depth of the flood waters, we have these interesting verses regarding the duration of the flood. Genesis 7:24 says, "And the waters prevailed on the earth one hundred and fifty days"—about five months! Genesis 8:3 says, "At the end of the hundred and fifty days the waters decreased."

Genesis 8:4-5 tells us that "the ark rested in the seventh month, the seventeenth day of the month, on the mountains of Ararat." The waters continued to decrease until the tenth month. On the first day of the tenth month, "the tops of the mountains were seen." It took about seventy-five days for the tops of the mountains to be seen! This argues against a merely local flood.

According to Genesis 8:13-14, the flood waters had disappeared from the earth after 317 days (cf. 7:11 and 8:13) and the earth was completely dried after 375 days (cf. 7:11 and 8:14). The flood prevailed on the earth for 150 days, and it took 225 days for the earth to be dry. It is difficult to imagine that length of time if this were merely a local flood.

Where would all the water come from? Even though the Bible says that it rained for forty days and forty nights (Genesis 7:12), it would be difficult to prove that the great volume of water necessary to drown the entire planet would come from rain clouds. Some scientists and theologians have argued for a vapor canopy around the earth that collapsed at the time of the flood. They draw this conclusion from the statements in Genesis 1:6-7 about the "waters which were above the firmament [or expanse]." Since it apparently did not rain on the planet until the time of the flood, this vapor canopy would produce a tropical paradise all over the globe. This ended at the time of the flood, and the volume of water upon the earth was the result of the collapse of this canopy.

While this is a possibility, it is not necessary to prove the point. In the ocean depths of planet earth, scientists tell us that over two hundred million cubic miles of water are stored. That is enough water to drown the entire globe! Genesis 7:11 presents these facts to us:

> **In the six hundredth year of Noah's life, in the second month, the seventeenth day of the month, on that day all the fountains of the great deep were broken up, and the windows of heaven were opened.**

If we are reading the biblical account carefully, "all the fountains of the great deep" that were "broken up" continued to do so for five months (see 7:24-8:3). Such geological upheavals in the ocean depths cannot be reconciled with a local flood. The violent upheaval of oceanic waters could only be stopped by the hand of God Himself.

The Bible suggests that the flood waters necessary to cover the entire planet came from the ocean and that they receded into these giant storehouses and will never again be used to cover the globe. All floods from that point until now are indeed local floods, the result of heavy rains and the overflowing of rivers.

The dimensions of the ark. Could ancient man build a boat that would survive the violent upheaval of the oceans and the flood waters that continued their violent movements for 150 days? Genesis 6:14-16 describes this ark:

> **¹⁴Make yourself an ark of gopherwood; make rooms in the ark, and cover it inside and outside with pitch. ¹⁵And this is how you shall make it: The length of the ark shall be three hundred cubits, its width fifty cubits, and its height thirty cubits. ¹⁶You shall make a window for the ark, and you shall finish it to a cubit from above; and set the door of the ark in its side. You shall make it with lower, second, and third decks.**

Quite a barge! Three hundred cubits long, fifty cubits wide, and thirty cubits high. But how long is a cubit? The Babylonians had a "royal" cubit of 19.8 inches; the Egyptians had a short one of 17.6 inches and a long one of 20.65 inches. The Hebrews had a common cubit of 17.5 inches and a long one of 20.4 inches. A cubit, as far as we can ascertain, averages about one and a half feet, or 18 inches. This means that the ark was 450 feet long, 75 feet wide, and 45 feet high. It is one and one-half football fields long! (For your interest, the Queen Mary is 975 feet long, over twice as long as Noah's ark!)

With three decks (6:16), its deck areas would include over ninety-five thousand square feet. Its tonnage would be fourteen thousand tons, and its cubic foot space 1,400,000 cubic feet. The very size of this structure seems meaningless if the flood was merely a local event.

The description by the apostle Peter. The remarks of the apostle Peter in 2 Peter 3:4-6 seem to demand a worldwide catastrophe.

He states that the "world that then existed perished, being flooded with water." In verse 5 he speaks of the earth "standing out of water and in the water."

Peter's subsequent remarks about the coming destruction of the planet by fire seems to necessitate a worldwide flood in Noah's day (cf. 2 Peter 3:7 and 10-12). The fire will not be local. The future destruction is not limited to one country or geographical area of the planet. Since it is being compared to the destruction of Noah's day, it only seems logical to argue for a worldwide destruction in the time of Noah.

The destruction of the human race. How can a local flood cover the details of the Bible concerning the destruction of the entire human race? Only eight people survived out of a population numbering into the millions! Consider these statements:

> Matthew 24:39—"the flood came and took them all away"

> Luke 17:27—"the flood came and destroyed them all"

> 1 Peter 3:20—"in which a few, that is, eight souls, were saved through water"

> 2 Peter 2:5—"did not spare the ancient world . . . bringing in the flood on the world of the ungodly"

> 2 Peter 3:6—"the world that then existed perished"

In Genesis 6:17 God says He would "destroy from under heaven all flesh in which is the breath of life; and everything that is on the earth shall die." Genesis 7:21-23 gives this summary of the destruction:

> **²¹And all flesh died that moved on the earth: birds and cattle and beasts and every creeping thing that creeps on the earth, and every man. ²²All in whose nostrils was the breath of the spirit of life, all that was on the dry land, died. ²³So He destroyed all living things which were on the face of the ground: both man and cattle, creeping thing and bird of the air. They were destroyed from the earth. Only Noah and those who were with him in the ark remained alive.**

That argues for a worldwide, global catastrophe!

The Biological Issue

People often use the problem of the animals to deny the accuracy and reliability of the Genesis account of the flood. Could the animals fit into the ark and could they survive? Let's take a look at what Genesis 6:19-21 says:

> [19]**"And of every living thing of all flesh you shall bring two of every sort into the ark, to keep them alive with you; they shall be male and female. [20]Of the birds after their kind, of animals after their kind, and of every creeping thing of the earth after its kind, two of every kind will come to you to keep them alive. [21]And you shall take for yourself of all food that is eaten, and you shall gather it to yourself; and it shall be food for you and for them."**

Additional instruction is found in Genesis 7:2-3, 8-9, and 14-16:

> [2]**"You shall take with you seven each of every clean animal, a male and his female; two each of animals that are unclean, a male and his female; [3]also seven each of birds of the air, male and female, to keep the species alive on the face of all the earth."**

> [8]**Of clean beasts, of beasts that are unclean, of birds, and of everything that creeps on the earth, [9]two by two they went into the ark to Noah, male and female, as God had commanded Noah.**

> [14]**. . . they and every beast after its kind, all cattle after their kind, every creeping thing that creeps on the earth after its kind, and every bird after its kind, every bird of every sort. [15]And they went into the ark to Noah, two by two, of all flesh in which is the breath of life. [16]So those that entered, male and female of all flesh, went in as God had commanded him; and the LORD shut him in.**

Ernst Mayr, a leading American systematic taxonomist, lists one million species, including mammals, birds, reptiles, amphibians, fishes, echinoderms, arthropods, mollusks, worms, coelenterates, sponges, and protozoans. There would be no need to make provision for many of these species since they could survive in the water. The total number of species of mammals, birds, reptiles, and amphibians in Mayr's listings is 17,600. The original "kinds" described in the Bible may have been far less.

The size of the ark with its three deck areas could easily have contained the animals which the Bible says went into the ark. But could those animals survive? The biblical text tells us that Noah was instructed to provide enough food (6:21). It is possible that hibernation and estivation could have been used by God to help these animals survive.

How could Noah gather them all into the ark? That process alone seems impossible to achieve. But the Bible does not say that Noah had to search for them and "round them up." *God* instructed the animals to go into the ark. Genesis 6:20 says they "will come to you"; Genesis 7:15 says, "And they went into the ark to Noah." God caused the animals to come to Noah; he did not have to go and search for them.

Obviously, this requires us to believe in biological miracles. The Bible speaks of a great fish swallowing Jonah—do you believe that happened? It tells us of the shutting of the mouths of lions in the days of Daniel—do you believe that occurred? And what about the physical, bodily resurrection of Jesus Christ—did that really happen? The Bible is filled with accounts of the supernatural, the miraculous. We should not be surprised that God performed a miracle to get all the animals into the ark.

The Historical Issue

It is one thing to examine the biblical account of this global catastrophe in which the first human civilization was destroyed; it is another thing to ask if there is any other evidence for such a disaster in the pages of history or in the artifacts of archaeological discovery.

Interestingly, flood stories appear in over forty different ancient cultures. Their accounts are filled with mythological and fanciful details not found in the biblical record, but the presence of these stories lends credence to the validity of the biblical record. History does reveal the evidence of a tremendous flood long ago that affected many cultures of the world.

The evidence from fossil remains in the strata of earth's surface also argues for a global catastrophe. Tropical vegetation in the mouths of large mammals buried in the ice of Siberia lends support to a worldwide disaster, changing the atmospheric conditions of the planet. The so-called Ice Age may in fact be one of the evidences for a global flood as described in the book of Genesis. There is much to convince a person of catastrophe in ancient history.

The Spiritual Issue

Why did God bring such a disaster upon the world? Why did He destroy the first human civilization? The Bible is clear that this was His goal and purpose and that the flood accomplished His desire. But why?

To reveal His mighty power. God's supernatural power is displayed majestically and powerfully through the global catastrophe He brought to this world long ago. His power is evident as He controls the forces of nature, bringing up the great volumes of water from the ocean caverns and depths, and then making the waters recede by causing a wind to blow over the earth.

Psalm 148:8 speaks of the elements obeying God's word: "Fire and hail, snow and clouds; Stormy wind, fulfilling His word." It was His simple word that brought this great disaster. Second Peter 3:5 makes an important point about creation when it says, "by the word of God the heavens were of old, and the earth standing out of water and in the water." Verse 7 says that "the heavens and the earth which now exist are kept in store by the same word, reserved for fire until the day of judgment and perdition of ungodly men." God simply spoke the worlds into existence, and by His word the flood waters rose to cover the highest mountains of the planet.

To reveal His righteous punishment of the wicked. Second Peter 2:5 says that God "did not spare the ancient world." It states that He brought the "flood on the world of the ungodly." Verse 9 says that "the Lord knows how to deliver the godly out of temptations and to reserve the unjust under punishment for the day of judgment."

The wicked society of Noah's day was ripe for the judgment of God. It was a righteous act on His part (Psalm 119:137; 145:17). It is extremely fallacious thinking to suppose that we can escape the judgment of God. God's punishment of the wicked in Noah's day is a reminder to all of us that His judgment will inevitably come to all who refuse His gracious offer of salvation through His Son, Jesus Christ our Lord.

146

To reveal His wonderful protection of the believer. Noah, his wife, his three sons and their wives, eight people in all, escaped that terrible judgment because they were in the ark of safety (2 Peter 2:5). Peter assures us that "the Lord knows how to deliver the godly out of temptations" (2:9).

To reveal His loving patience toward us. First Peter 3:20 speaks of "the longsuffering [patience] of God" which "waited in the days of Noah, while the ark was being prepared, in which a few, that is eight souls, were saved through water." Second Peter 3:9 is a powerful verse on the patience of God:

> "The Lord is not slack concerning His promise, as some count slackness, but is longsuffering [patient] toward us, not willing that any should perish but that all should come to repentance."

The Lord is patient toward us because He does not want any one to perish but all of us to come to repentance. God's patience was demonstrated in the days of Noah, giving that generation 120 years to repent and believe. The reason for the delay (from our perspective) in the second coming of Jesus Christ is God's patience—He is bringing to Himself a great host of people who will believe in Him and "come to repentance." That's why Jesus Christ has not yet returned.

To reveal His special purpose for the people of God who await the second coming of Jesus Christ. Matthew 24:36-44 speaks of the relationship of Noah's day to the day when Jesus Christ will return:

> "But of that day and hour no one knows, no, not even the angels of heaven, but My Father only. But as the days of Noah were, so also will the coming of the Son of Man be. For as in the days before the flood, they were eating and drinking, marrying and giving in marriage, until the day that Noah entered the ark, and did not know until the flood came and took them all away, so also will the coming of the Son of Man be. Then two men will be in the field: one will be taken and the other left. Two women will be grinding at the mill: one will be taken and the other left. Watch therefore, for you do not know what hour your Lord is coming. But know this, that if the master of the house had known what hour the thief would come, he would

147

have watched and not allowed his house to be broken into. Therefore you also be ready, for the Son of Man is coming at an hour when you do not expect Him."

The special purpose of God is clearly stated for the believer who looks back to the days of Noah and contemplates the meaning of that whole disaster:

24:42—"Watch therefore, for you do not know what hour your Lord is coming."

24:44—"Therefore you also be ready, for the Son of Man is coming at an hour when you do not expect Him."

Watch and be ready—that's the lesson to be learned from the global catastrophe of Noah's day.

Civilization Starts Over Again

Following this global disaster, God remembers Noah and makes a covenant with him (Genesis 9:15-16):

15"And I will remember My covenant which is between Me and you and every living creature of all flesh; the waters shall never again become a flood to destroy all flesh. 16The rainbow shall be in the cloud, and I will look on it to remember the everlasting covenant between God and every living creature of all flesh that is on the earth."

The rainbow is a reminder of the faithfulness of God, His promise never to destroy the earth with a flood as He did in the days of Noah.

When Noah and his family came out of the ark, it is interesting to observe what he immediately did. Genesis 8:20 says, "Noah built an altar to the LORD . . . and offered burnt offerings on the altar." The Bible indicates God's approval as it says in verse 21, "And the LORD smelled a soothing aroma." It pleased the Lord that Noah began life on earth with his family in an attitude of worship and commitment to Him.

Noah is an example to all of us of what commitment to the Lord really means. Genesis 6:22 says, "Thus Noah did; according to all that God commanded him, so he did." The same thought is repeated in Genesis 7:5, 9, and 16. Noah obeyed the Lord and did whatever he was told to do. Our world would be a better place if we all obeyed the Lord. Civilization succeeds when it is obedient to God. It destroys itself quickly when it departs from the laws and commandments of God. Civilization becomes corrupt and violent when it is not obedient to God, and it becomes ripe for God's judgment. It seems that such a day has arrived again on the scene of human history.

Civilization begins again with clear instruction from God about the sanctity of human life. In Genesis 9:6 we read:

> **"Whoever sheds man's blood,**
> **By man his blood shall be shed;**
> **For in the image of God**
> **He made man."**

This command is a return to creation and its truth. We were made "in the image of God and after His likeness." One of the ten commandments (Exodus 20:13) states, "You shall not murder." We have no right to take another person's life. Government is instructed by God to bring capital punishment upon people who commit capital crimes. God has given the governing powers that right, a fact the New Testament affirms (Romans 13:1-5).

The new civilization is given the same command that God gave to Adam and Eve. God said to Noah and his sons, "Be fruitful and multiply, and fill the earth" (Genesis 9:1). Verse 7 repeats it:

> **"And as for you, be fruitful and multiply;**
> **Bring forth abundantly in the earth**
> **And multiply in it."**

God Delights in Multitudes of People

The first civilization wandered away from the Lord and His commands. It ended in tragedy. A global catastrophe brought the first civilization to an end, a demonstration of the power of God and our accountability to him. The next time it will be a judgment by fire, not by flood. That judgment will be equally awesome in its dimensions and destruction. It is coming. Our means of escape is the same as in the days of Noah—faith in the living God, protected by the ark of safety, our Lord Jesus Christ.

Have you settled your eternal destiny by putting your faith and trust in the death and resurrection of Jesus Christ? To live forever with the Lord requires faith in what He has done in dying on the cross for our sins, taking our place and paying the price for our wickedness and rebellion. His resurrection is the guarantee that we shall also live again. The Bible teaches that one day when Jesus Christ comes again, the dead will be resurrected. Those with faith in the Person and work of Jesus Christ our Savior and Lord will live forever with the Lord. Those who reject Him will spend eternity without God, without hope, in a place God calls hell, the place of eternal punishment (Matthew 25:46).

Romans 10:9-10 makes it clear what we must do to be saved from God's righteous judgment:

> That if you confess with your mouth the Lord Jesus and believe in your heart that God has raised Him from the dead, you will be saved. For with the heart one believes to righteousness, and with the mouth confession is made to salvation.

Final Observations

The study of Genesis from creation to the flood gives us some important understanding and insights to govern and direct our lives in the present day. Our study of the biblical account has revealed the following:

1. The physical and material universe was created by God in six days.

2. The days of creation appear to be twenty-four-hour days.

3. The human body was formed by God from the dust of the ground and lives because of the creative breath of Almighty God.

4. Marriage is a commitment by a man and a woman to have sex only with each other and to bring forth children as a result of that sexual union.

5. Satan (the devil) tempted Eve and persuaded her to disobey God; Adam deliberately disobeyed and was not deceived.

6. Humanity is morally helpless because of the fall of Adam and Eve, and all persons in subsequent human history are born with sinful natures.

7. Spiritual death occurred the day Adam and Eve sinned, and their physical death was a consequence.

8. The hope of humanity is the Seed of the woman, a

Person Who will defeat Satan and bring life to all who will believe.

9. Human life is sacred because we were made in the image of God, and the premeditated, deliberate act of murder demands the death penalty as a consequence.

10. Longevity in the first human civilization resulted in an ability to bear children in greater numbers and over longer periods of time than is possible today. The result was a population in the millions at the time of the flood.

11. Demonic activity was present in the pre-flood civilization, producing a corrupt and violent society that deserved the judgment of God.

12. The flood was a global disaster, resulting in the death of all living things with the exception of Noah, his wife, his three sons and their wives, and the animals taken into the ark.

13. The rainbow is a reminder of God's promise never to destroy the world with a flood. The next time God executes global judgment it will be with fire.

14. The global catastrophe of the Genesis flood is a warning to all of us–we are to watch and be ready for the second coming of Jesus Christ.

Bibliography

Allis, Oswald T. *The Five Books of Moses.* Philadelphia: The Presbyterian and Reformed Publishing Co., 1949.

Archer, Gleason. *A Survey of Old Testament Introduction.* Chicago: Moody Press, 1964.

Barnhouse, Donald G. *Genesis.* 2 vols. Grand Rapids: Zondervan Publishing House, 1971.

Baxter, J. Sidlow. *Explore the Book.* Vol. 1. Grand Rapids: Zondervan Publishing House, 1960.

Berkouwer, G. C. *Man: The Image of God.* Grand Rapids: Wm. B. Eerdmans Publishing Co., 1962.

Brooks, Keith L. *The Riches of Genesis.* Los Angeles: Brooks Publishers, 1936.

Carroll, B. H. *Studies in Genesis.* Nashville: Broadman Press, 1937.

Clark, Harold W. *Genesis and Science.* Nashville: Southern Publishing Association, 1967.

Cole, Glen G. *Creation and Science.* Cincinnati: Standard Publishing Co., 1927.

Cummings, Violet M. *Noah's Ark: Fact or Fable?* San Diego: Creation-Science Research Center, 1972.

Custance, Arthur C. *Genesis and Early Man.* Grand Rapids: Zondervan Publishing House, 1975.

Bibliography

Davies, G. Henton. *Genesis.* The Broadman Bible Commentary, Vol. 1. Nashville: Broadman Press, 1969.

Davis, John J. *Paradise to Prison.* Grand Rapids: Baker Book House, 1975.

DeHaan, M. R. *Genesis and Evolution.* Grand Rapids: Zondervan Publishing House, 1962.

Delitzsch, Franz. *A New Commentary on Genesis.* Edinburgh: T. & T. Clark, 1899.

Elliott, Ralph H. *The Message of Genesis.* Nashville: Broadman Press, 1961.

Erdman, Charles R. *The Book of Genesis.* Old Tappan, N.J.: Fleming H. Revell Publishing Co., 1950.

Evans, William. *Genesis.* New York: Fleming H. Revell Publishing Co., 1916.

Filby, Frederick A. *Creation Revealed: A Study of Genesis 1 in the Light of Modern Science.* Westwood, N. J.: Fleming H. Revell Publishing Co., 1964.

————. *The Flood Reconsidered.* Grand Rapids: Zondervan Publishing House, 1970.

Free, Joseph P. *Archaeology and Bible History.* Wheaton, Ill.: Scripture Press, 1959.

Gish, Duane T. and Donald H. Rohrer, eds. *Up with Creation!* San Diego: Creation-Life Publishers, 1978.

Gordon, Alex R. *The Early Traditions of Genesis.* Edinburgh: T. & T. Clark, 1907.

Gruber, L. Franklin. *The Six Creative Days.* Burlington: Lutheran Literary Board, 1941.

Harris, R. Laird. *Man: God's Eternal Creation.* Chicago: Moody Press, 1971.

Harrison, R. K. *Introduction to the Old Testament.* Grand Rapids: Wm. B. Eerdmans Publishing Co., 1969.

Henry, Matthew. *Matthew Henry's Commentary on the Whole Bible.* Vol. 1. Old Tappan, N.J.: Revell H. Revell Publishing Co., n.d.

Hopkins, Garland E. *The Mighty Beginnings.* St. Louis: The Bethany Press, 1956.

Lammerts, Walter E. *Why Not Creation?* Grand Rapids: Baker Book House, 1970.

Lange, John P. *Genesis.* Translated by T. Lewis and A. Gosman. New York: Charles Scribner and Co., 1868.

Leupold, H. C. *Exposition of Genesis.* Grand Rapids: Baker Book House, 1950.

Lever, Jan. *Creation and Evolution.* Grand Rapids: Grand Rapids International Publications, 1958.

Luther, Martin. *Luther's Commentary on Genesis.* Grand Rapids: Zondervan Publishing House, 1958.

Mackintosh, C. H. *Notes on the Book of Genesis.* New York: Loizeaux Brothers, 1880.

Montgomery, John W. *The Quest for Noah's Ark.* Minneapolis: Bethany Christian Fellowship, 1972.

Morgan, G. Campbell. *Genesis.* The Analyzed Bible, vol. 1. New York: Fleming H. Revell Publishing Co., 1911.

Morris, Henry M. *The Twilight of Evolution.* Grand Rapids: Baker Book House, 1963.

————. *Evolution and the Modern Christian.* Philadelphia: The Presbyterian and Reformed Publishing Co., 1967.

————. *Scientific Creationism.* San Diego: Creation-Life Publishers, 1974.

————. *The Genesis Record.* San Diego: Creation-Life Publishers, 1976.

Nelson, Byron C. *The Deluge Story in Stone.* Minneapolis: Bethany Fellowship, 1968.

Niles, D. T. *Studies on Genesis.* Philadelphia: The Westminster Press, 1958.

Owen, G. Frederick. *Archaeology and the Bible.* Westwood, N. J.: Fleming H. Revell Publishing Co., 1961.

Patten, Donald W. *The Biblical Flood and the Ice Epoch.* Seattle: Pacific Meridian Publishing Co., 1966.

Bibliography

Payne, D. F. *Genesis One Reconsidered.* Carol Stream, Ill.: Tyndale House, 1964.

Pember, G. H. *Earth's Earliest Ages.* London: Hodder and Stoughton, 1907.

Pfeiffer, Charles F. *The Book of Genesis.* Grand Rapids: Baker Book House, 1958.

Pilkey, John. *The Origin of the Nations.* San Diego: Master Book Publishers, 1984.

Pink, Arthur W. *Gleanings in Genesis.* Chicago: Moody Press, 1922.

Ramm, Bernard. *The Christian View of Science and Scripture.* Grand Rapids: Wm. B. Eerdmans Publishing Co., 1954.

Rehwinkel, Alfred M. *The Flood.* St. Louis: Concordia Publishing House, 1951.

Ross, Hugh. *The Cosmic Fingerprint.* Orange, Calif.: Promise Publishing Co., 1988.

Ryle, Herbert E. *The Early Narratives of Genesis.* London: Macmillan and Co., 1892.

Schaeffer, Francis A. *Genesis in Space and Time.* Downers Grove, Ill.: InterVarsity Press, 1972.

Slusher, Harold S. *Critique of Radiometric Dating.* San Diego: Institute for Creation Research, 1973.

Velikovsky, Immanuel. *Earth in Upheaval.* New York: Doubleday and Co., 1955.

Vos, Howard F. *Genesis and Archaeology.* Chicago: Moody Press, 1963.

Whitcomb, John C. *The Early Earth.* Winona Lake, Ind.: BMH Books, 1972.

Whitcomb, John C. and Henry M. Morris. *The Genesis Flood.* Philadelphia: The Presbyterian and Reformed Publishing Co., 1961.

Wilder-Smith, A. E. *Man's Origin, Man's Destiny.* Wheaton, Ill.: Harold Shaw Publishers, 1968.

————. *The Natural Sciences Know Nothing of Evolution.* San Diego: Master Books, 1981.

Wiseman, P. J. *Creation Revealed in Six Days.* London: Marshall, Morgan and Scott, 1949.

Wright, G. Ernest, ed. *The Bible and the Ancient Near East.* New York: Doubleday and Co., 1961.

————. *Biblical Archaeology.* Philadelphia: The Westminster Press, 1957.

Yates, Kyle M. *Genesis.* The Wycliffe Bible Commentary, ed. Charles F. Pfeiffer and Everett F. Harrison. Chicago: Moody Press, 1962.

Young, E. J. *Studies in Genesis One.* Philadelphia: The Presbyterian and Reformed Publishing Co., 1964.

Zlotowitz, Rabbi Meir. *Bereishis.* Vol. 1. New York: Mesorah Publications, Ltd., 1977.